D1567463

Fly Fishing for Saltwater's Finest

JOHN N. COLE
BRAD BURNS

Human Kinetics

Library of Congress Cataloging-in-Publication Data

Cole, John, 1923-
    Fly fishing for saltwater's finest / John Cole and Brad Burns.
      p.   cm.
    ISBN 0-7360-0130-1
    1. Saltwater fly fishing.   2. Marine fishes--East (U.S.) I. Burns, Brad. II. Title.
    SH456.2.C66   2000
    799.1'6--dc21   99-053766
                                                          CIP

ISBN: 0-7360-0130-1

Acquisitions Editor: Martin Barnard; **Managing Editor**: Leigh LaHood; **Copyeditor**: Bob Replinger; **Proofreader**: Andrew Smith; **Indexer**: Betty Frizzell; **Graphic Designer**: Robert Reuther; **Graphic Artist**: Sandra Meier; **Cover Designer**: Jack W. Davis; **Photographer (cover)**: © David Brownell; **Photographer (interior)**: photo on page 23 by Dick White; all other photos by Brad Burns; **Illustrator**: John Rice; **Printer**: Versa Press; Dekker

Excerpt on pages 121-122 reprinted with permission from Nathaniel Pryor Reed III.

Excerpt on pages 122-123 reprinted with permission from Jeffrey Cardenas, 1995, *Marquesa: A Time and Place With Fish*. (Far Hills, NJ: Meadow Run Press).

Human Kinetics books are available at special discounts for bulk purchase. Special editions or book excerpts can also be created to specification. For details, contact the Special Sales Manager at Human Kinetics.

Printed in the United States of America

10 9 8 7 6 5 4 3 2 1

Human Kinetics
Web site: http://www.humankinetics.com/

United States: Human Kinetics
P.O. Box 5076, Champaign, IL 61825-5076
1-800-747-4457
e-mail: humank@hkusa.com

Canada: Human Kinetics
475 Devonshire Road Unit 100, Windsor, ON N8Y 2L5
1-800-465-7301 (in Canada only)
e-mail: humank@hkcanada.com

Europe: Human Kinetics
P.O. Box IW14, Leeds LS16 6TR, United Kingdom
+44 (0)113-278 1708
e-mail: humank@hkeurope.com

Australia: Human Kinetics
57A Price Avenue, Lower Mitcham, South Australia 5062
(08) 82771555
e-mail: liahka@senet.com.au

New Zealand: Human Kinetics
P.O. Box 105-231, Auckland Central
09-523-3462
e-mail: humank@hknewz.com

Fly Fishing
for
Saltwater's
Finest

Contents

Contents

Introduction

Capt. Jeffrey Cardenas, my Key West friend and fishing companion for more than a decade, has been casting flies to saltwater fish for more than 20 years now. He has been a professional fishing guide, an explorer of new and exotic saltwater fly-fishing places, a creator of some of the finest saltwater fishing flies, and the proprietor of one of the nation's friendliest and most comprehensively stocked saltwater fly-fishing retail and mail-order stores.

He must have cast flies to five thousand tarpon over those years. You might think that the process would have become routine. Listen to what he has to say after all these years and then judge whether his fishing has lost its magic.

"When an angler whose previous fish of a lifetime was a 20-inch rainbow walks into my shop after hooking an 80-pound tarpon, I can see the electricity jumping off his skin.

"My personal evolution in the sport has allowed me a great deal of time on the water, but every time an 80-pound tarpon takes my fly, I still feel the electricity jumping off my skin."

Another lifelong friend, Peter Cox, cast his first saltwater fly from the rocky ledges of his Maine-coast home just a few years ago. He was, to put it mildly, immediately addicted. Why?

"For one thing," he explains, "there's the culture. I like being with other fly fishers because they share my enthusiasm. For another, I know I'll never master the sport. There is always something new to learn—how fish hang in the water, where they feed at a particular time of day on a particular tide. And when there are those fishless days, you know a perfect cast will be as satisfying as hooking a fish. Even if you don't catch anything, you've had a fine day fishing."

Two anglers, one in the nation's southernmost community, another on the far northeast shores of Maine; one a fly fisher for more than three decades, the other a relative beginner. Yet both are fascinated, thrilled, and yes, addicted to the activity. And they are far from alone. Over the past decade or more, the number of saltwater fly fishers—men and women—has grown incrementally each year. And it's still growing. Everywhere, from the northernmost coastal communities of downeast Maine, along the convoluted shores and windswept islands of Maine's New England neighbors, past the rips off

Introduction

Montauk, the sweep of New Jersey's superb sand beaches, the Chesapeake and the barrier islands of the southern states, on beyond the length of Florida's two coasts and the Gulf's semitropical waters off the panhandle, Louisiana and Texas—wherever salt waters flow you'll find fly fishers.

They come for the electricity Jeffrey Cardenas knows so well. They come for the fulfillment of that one splendid cast that Peter Cox discovered. And they come in anticipation of meeting the most challenging, strongest, and loveliest creatures of the seas—the fish that take saltwater flies.

It is, all of it, a magnificent adventure. Who can claim that sliding a 15-pound striper onto the grassy bank of a solitary Maine marsh is more memorable than watching the scimitar tail of a 30-pound permit break the silken surface of a tidal flat as the great fish tilts to eat your fly? The question is not relevant, for all saltwater fly fishing holds such moments, moments that will sustain your finest memories for the full span of your years.

We do not claim, then, that these pages decribe the only 10 worthy fly-fishing venues on the coast. Nor do we claim that the fish we nominate for excellence are the only superior creatures that swim. No, saltwater fly fishing is too rich, too extravagant in its offerings to be so exclusionary.

What we have done is select 10 venues and 10 species that we have found fulfilling over the years. For when you combine the angling experience of this book's two authors, you'll come close to 100 years in as many different fishing locations. That's a lot to look back at—a great sea of memories. It takes some hard thinking to pick out the best.

But that's what we've tried to do; that's been our challenge. In the process, we are sharing every bit of the experience with you. The coast from Maine to Texas comprises thousands of miles, and they're all yours. That's part of what makes saltwater fly fishing so splendid. All of it can be good. What we have done is choose 10 places and 10 fish that promise greatness.

The rest is up to you.

PART I

Preparing for Saltwater Fly Fishing

SOME YEARS AGO I WAS FISHING WITH A FRIEND NEAR PORT O'CONNOR, TEXAS. Our plan was to fish for the schools of redfish that lived in the shallow, saltwater lakes in back of the barrier beaches. Because these fish seldom are larger than 28 or 30 inches, an eight-weight fly rod is more than adequate. That equipment, rigged with a 12-pound-test leader and a popping bug, was what I held in my hand. Moving between fishing spots, we crossed a pass that opened into the Gulf of Mexico; despite the hot, windless day the evidence of the ocean's restlessness was visible all around us. A wrecked shrimp dragger lay on its side near the beach at the mouth of the pass, a victim of shifting sand bars, rapid currents, and large waves. Only the pilothouse and part of the rigging stood above the water. "It will be all gone soon," said my companion. "The pass has moved east several hundred yards in just the last few years." Where large commercial boats had once passed through to the sea, a fully vegetated beach and dune, a regular island, was now grazed by cattle and nested upon by the incredible number and variety of the area's shorebirds.

Looking down the beach my eyes caught the glint of sunlight on the white undersides of a flock of pelicans as they milled over a patch of disturbed water. When the boat drew closer, the disturbance materialized into a school of 40- to 50-pound jack crevalle, feeding on mullet. Shoals of the frantic mullet leapt from the water amidst whirlpools the size of a pickup truck's hood—whirlpools caused by the tails of the powerful jacks. Unlike any fish except maybe a barracuda, jacks have a distinct expression on their faces; it's a scowl, a big, mean, hateful scowl. I could see the black eyeballs of the predators, focused and determined, as they lashed at their prey.

It was into the middle of this living maelstrom that I cast my little popper. On the second or third pop, one of those scowling faces emerged from a huge boil, and the fly simply disappeared. I'm not sure if the jack bolted when it felt the hook or simply raced off after another mullet, but despite my careful attempts to avoid being broken off, so great was the force of the jack's strike that the tippet parted on impact. A few minutes later I was retied, but the jacks and mullet had gone down. All that remained were a few pelicans paddling around, hoping for a crippled mullet to float to the surface.

Such is the potential variety and excitement of saltwater fly fishing, and the demands placed on the fly caster and his or her tackle. It's not that it's superior to freshwater fishing; it's just different, different among other ways in its scale. The saltwater environment remains unconfined and wild. Fish don't just aggregate in an area, they often travel in schools—upon occasion thousands of fish move together, some as predator, many more as prey. Fish must be tough to live in such a place. Saltwater game fish are firmed by their daily battles with tides, waves, and predators. They're nourished by a food chain that extends through many levels, ensuring that almost no fish is truly safe from something bigger, or faster, or with more teeth. All this can take place within sight, even within a rock's throw, of this country's most populated areas. This is the lure of saltwater fishing. Those who have discovered the thrill of feeling the take of a powerful fish through a taut fly line or the satisfaction of seducing a wild creature with a fly cast manually and tied by hand find no better way exists to fish the salt than with a fly rod.

What do we need to know to prepare for saltwater fly fishing? What do we need for tackle, for knots, leaders, flies? How is saltwater fly fishing different from fishing lakes and streams? Part I will answer these questions and prepare you for your foray into saltwater fly fishing. In part II we'll cover 10 of the great inshore saltwater fly-rod game fish and their top locations. When you're finished you'll have a good idea of what it takes to fly fish in saltwater, what some of your area's best targets might be, and where and how to go after them.

Chapter

1

Reading the Water

*F*rom even experienced freshwater fly fishers comes the question and lament, "How do I get started; the ocean is so huge?" Yes, the ocean is immense, but the fisher can break it into pieces and analyze each for its fishability. Done in this way reading an area of saltwater is similar to reading a trout stream or a bass lake.

Tides

One big difference between freshwater and saltwater environments is tides. In their simplest terms, tides are changes in the height of ocean waters—flood for rising water levels and ebb for declining water levels—caused by the gravity of the moon and sun, and the revolution of the earth. Tides, however, can be complicated events. Although tide tables predict the times of high and low water in a particular place, winds and the inflow of freshwater can seriously affect the accuracy of projected water depths and current movements. No table can predict their influences. Tide tables show the time for high or low tides each day, as well as the rise of the high tide above mean low water levels. They also show the deviation of a particular low tide from those same mean low water levels. The table is usually created for a major port, and a separate attachment provides time and magnitude differences in several nearby locations. See figure 1.1 for an example of a tide table.

Navigational charts go hand in hand with tide tables. A navigational chart produced by NOAA, the National Oceanic and Atmospheric Administration, is really an ocean map that shows the mean low water depth in many locations over the bottom. It also shows what the bottom is made of, how it is

```
Portland, Maine
Tide Predictions (High and Low Waters)      March, 1999
NOAA, National Ocean Service

Standard Time

Day        Time     Ht.      Time      Ht.      Time     Ht.      Time      Ht.

1   M      411am L   -.1     1026am H  10.4     444pm L   -.8     1058pm H   9.7
2   Tu     457am L   -.3     1111am H  10.4     526pm L   -.7     1139pm H   9.7
3   W      540am L   -.3     1152am H  10.2     605pm L   -.5
4   Th     1217am H   9.7     620am L   -.2     1232pm H   9.9      643pm L   -.2
5   F      1254am H   9.6     700am L    .0      111pm H   9.6      719pm L    .1
6   Sa     130am H    9.4     740am L    .3      151pm H   9.1      757pm L    .5
7   Su     208am H    9.1     821am L    .6      233pm H   8.7      836pm L   1.0
```

Figure 1.1   *This is a tide table for Portland, Maine, during March 1999. On Monday, March 1, tide was low at 4:11 A.M. The tide was .1 feet below normal. Tide was then high again at 10:26 A.M., reaching a height of 10.4 feet above the normal low tide depth reflected on a nautical chart for the area. Reprinted from http://www.opsd.nos.noaa.gov.*

shaped, how fast and in which direction currents flow during flood and ebb tides, and a variety of other information important to both fishing and boating.

All predatory fish position themselves to take advantage of existing conditions. Just as a trout rests behind a boulder, in a lie that gives it a vantage point from which to jump out and eat unsuspecting minnows, so a striped bass may rest behind the jagged tip of a submerged ledge, waiting to feed on herring swept along by the currents of an ebbing tide. By understanding a few basic feeding-station scenarios, you can make the most of the conditions that you may come across while fishing.

Structures and Moving Water

Most predatory fish like to position themselves behind structures being swept by moving water (see figure 1.2). The structure can be as small as a six-inch rise on a sandy bottom. Any structure that causes an abrupt change in the depth of moving water will create places where currents form back eddies—places where water slows, or in some cases moves backward. These resting places are often directly adjacent to the rapid flow caused by the constriction that the structure has made in the water column. The fish can survey the rapid water, looking for baitfish without the exertion of bucking turbulent currents.

Figure 1.2   *Like a huge trout, this striper lies in the back eddy behind this boulder.*

The predator gathers the same advantage from positioning itself in a current seam, shown in figure 1.3. A seam is a line of turbulence caused by the meeting of two bodies of water moving at different speeds. A rapidly draining tidal creek entering a slower moving river creates seams on both sides of its current flow. A predator can wait in the confused waters of the seam to snatch bait disadvantaged by the faster moving creek outflow.

Figure 1.3   *A seam holds fish because it provides a window into fast water, but it also allows the predator to hold its position with minimum effort.*

Inlets

Often the advantages of structures and seams are combined in inlets. Inlets are the passages between protected waters and more-open waters, including the open ocean. The protected waters often contain shallow nursery grounds that harbor small baitfish. Predators of all types use the seams and feeding stations of submerged structures within the inlet to bushwhack the weaker swimmers passing in and out of the inlet with the tides. Figure 1.4 shows an inlet.

Edges

An edge is an area of transition from one general depth or condition of the water to another. In offshore angling it may cover hundreds of miles and be important because of what the different temperature or light level at that particular depth means to the baitfish. To the inshore fly fisher it may mean the edge of a submerged grass bed where weakfish patrol for wayward grass shrimp, or a broad drop-off along a flat where bonefish can wait comfortably

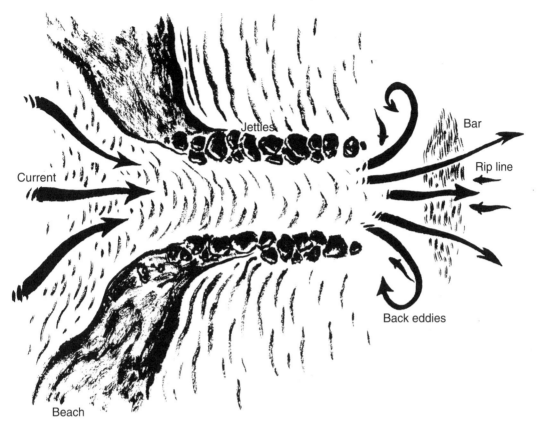

Figure 1.4 *Inlets/outlets are often top producers. The best fishing usually occurs where the current flow meets the open water.*

for baitfish evacuating the lowering water levels caused by an ebb tide (see figure 1.5).

Flats

Flats, or areas of shallow water, are often themselves broad feeding areas. Game fish may find that they are able to overtake or root from the bottom bait that is abundant and easy to catch. A flat may be a vast bay in Florida covered by turtle grass, a huge sandy stretch inside one of the Carolina sounds, or just a few acres of mud-bottomed cove along the coast of Maine where marine worms are vulnerable during their spawning activity. Game fish on flats often reveal their presence by disturbing the surface of the water (see figure 1.6). Sometimes they become visible with the help of polarized glasses.

How do you know which lump on the bottom holds fish at a particular time or which flat is frequented by bonefish? Ah! The perfect question. Certainly no structure, even the best one, always produces. With experience in a

Figure 1.5 *This bonefish waits in the security of deeper water for food to flush off the shallow flat with an ebb tide.*

Figure 1.6 *Redfish—and others—give themselves away while "tipping-up" or "tailing" on bottom forage.*

particular fishery you can look at a chart or examine a body of water and pick some likely feeding locations. Nothing, however, will replace the knowledge gained by years of observation or the experience that comes from tossing flies into all the likely looking spots in a given area at different times of the year, under different conditions of tide and weather. The chapters about individual fish contain a sort of case study on each species. When you've read them, you'll have much of the knowledge that you'll need to fish the subject area effectively. You'll also find that much of the information is transferable to other fishing scenarios. Although in many of these fisheries a boat is not necessary, it's essential to some and helpful in all. Boating, however, adds additional complication for those who want to undertake any of these fisheries on their own. Unless you're familiar with saltwater fly fishing and possess the right boat, I'd strongly suggest a guide, at least to begin with. A good guide—we'll discuss that in more depth in chapter 3—has made the casts that we talked about, has seen the area under a variety of conditions throughout the season, and has watched experienced anglers try their best to catch fish. A guide possesses the boat and equipment that will make your trip more comfortable and productive.

Chapter 2

Casting and Equipment

*T*o a large degree fly casting is fly casting. The techniques necessary to cast a fly accurately far out onto the water, especially in a hurry or in windy conditions, are the same for a 4-weight rod as they are for a 12-weight. In freshwater, however, fewer anglers develop into competent casters because they don't have to. In many, though not all, freshwater situations the fly need only be cast a few feet. Accuracy is important, but distance is not. In the chapters ahead you will see the advantage to being able to make a fly rod perform up to its potential. I have introduced some freshwater fly fishers to the salt who were quickly frustrated by their inability to capitalize on fishing opportunities because they couldn't cast beyond 30 feet. Part of their difficulty arose because many saltwater flies are larger and therefore more wind resistant than those used in freshwater. Casting these flies effectively requires a heavy-weight fly rod and good casting technique.

Saltwater Fly Casting

If you're going to fly cast in the salt you'll need to ask yourself a few questions: Can I handle a 9- or 10-weight rod? Can I false cast at least the entire head part of my fly line? Do I know how to double haul, to shoot line? Is my loop control good enough to cast effectively into a light wind? If your answer to all these questions is yes, then you're ready to attempt saltwater fly casting. If your answer to any of these questions is no, you're not alone. You can, however, do several things to prepare. First, if you know what kind of fishing you want to do, acquire rods of the proper weight and practice on the lawn. I'm constantly telling anglers new to saltwater fly fishing that the time to learn to cast is not when you're casting to fish. Buy an inexpensive line—because grass may hurt it—and learn to cast and control your outfit before you get near the water. Some fishing requires only that you cast when you see a fish; others require that you blind cast a 10-weight for hours. Most anglers will require some training. Some simple arm and shoulder exercises will help these muscles tremendously. I do some pushups and dumbbell exercises each winter, and enjoy it because I know it's preparation for fishing.

Get one of the professional casting instruction videos. Have a friend tape you casting and then study your movements compared with those on the video. This kind of preparation will go a long way when a 100-pound tarpon rolls 70 feet in front of the boat. Pay particular attention to casting in a tight loop. The formation of a tight loop means that you are applying the power of the casting stroke to a focused area—along a flat plane (see figure 2.1). A cast made with a tight loop will go much farther and present less surface area to the wind (see figure 2.2). You will also need to know how to double haul and how to shoot line. Watch the videos—seeing someone cast properly is more effective than reading about it.

Figure 2.1 *(a) The caster's wrist should travel in a straight line—as if it were on a track. (b) It may feel natural to move up then down, but it will ruin your cast.*

A fair amount of saltwater fishing is done with fast sinking-head lines that are rated in grains of weight rather than the normal line-numbering system. A 130-grain line is equivalent to a 4-weight line, a 300-grain line to a 10-weight, and a 500-grain line to a 12- or 13-weight. These lines easily carry a heavy fly through the air but can be difficult to cast. The reason for the difficulty is the momentum that resides in the heavy head. You're not likely to find any specialized instruction on casting heavy heads or bulky flies in casting

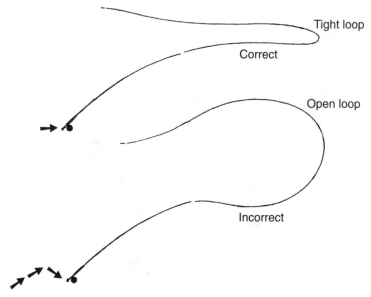

Figure 2.2   *The result of properly executing the cast, as in figure 2.1a, is a tight loop and greater line speed.*

instructional videos, so here are a couple of tips. To absorb the momentum of the head, you must cast the line with long arm movements that gradually—not abruptly—change the direction of the fly line, as shown in figure 2.3. You should avoid aerial false casting of these lines. Use a technique called the water haul, in which the fly lightly touches the water on every forward cast; this stops the heavy tip from swinging around and destroying the rhythm of the cast (see figure 2.4). Once mastered, the water haul also

Figure 2.3   *Long, smooth arm motions and changes of direction are necessary to cast heavy sinking heads.*

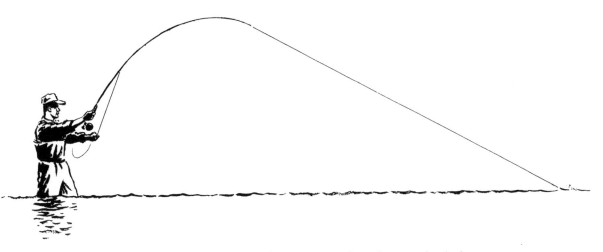

Figure 2.4 *Use the motions shown in figure 2.3 to perform the water haul. The water stops the line's forward motion and allows you to load the rod for the backcast.*

increases your casting productivity because even a moderate length of line touched to the water loads the rod for the backcast as if a much greater length of fly line was aerialized; you can make the casts with fewer rod strokes. This technique is also helpful in casting a bulky fly—even on a regular fly line—because it is hard to work out enough line to carry the bulky fly through the air by normal false casting.

Equipment

As fly casting is essentially fly casting, so saltwater fly fishing equipment is similar to that made for freshwater; the difference is really in the heavier duty nature of saltwater tackle.

Rods

For line weights of 7 or under few manufacturers offer special saltwater rods because the features found in purely saltwater rods are needed only where the size of fish and flies make larger rod weights necessary. Larger saltwater rods often have bigger guides because the lines—especially 11-, 12-, and 13-weight lines—are of a diameter that would cause enough resistance in smaller guides to limit casting distances severely. Grips are typically of the full wells type to give your hands a solid grip against the torque caused by loading a powerful rod for a long cast, and a butt extension is usually placed on the end of the reel seat for comfort and leverage (see figure 2.5). These, along with larger guides, are the only visible features separating saltwater from freshwater fly rods.

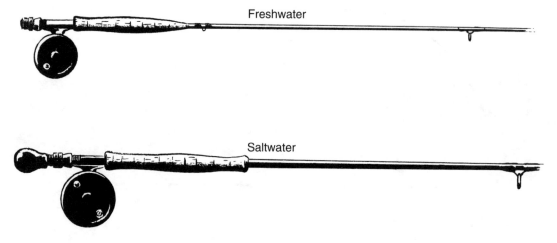

Figure 2.5 *The saltwater outfit often has a longer grip, extended butt, and a large, ceramic stripping guide.*

Debate rages among fly casters over the speed of the graphite used in modern fly rods. Some casters like a slower, more progressive rod. Others can't get one stiff and fast enough. For saltwater, the fans of fast-action rods are in the majority. I agree with them and feel that if you wish to slow down the rod just line it up one or two line sizes. You can certainly punch tight-looped casts into the wind much more efficiently with a fast-action rod.

Saltwater rods often are beefier in the butt than freshwater rods. This provides more lifting power on strong saltwater game fish. Even a moderately small saltwater game fish like a false albacore of 10 or 12 pounds can—like all members of the tuna family—turn on its side, and by the rapid beating of its sickle-shaped tail require unbelievable pressure to lift to the surface. I've caught these fish on a seven-weight and had to point the rod practically straight down into the water, eliminating almost all rod bend, to bring them to the boat (see figure 2.6). Excellent saltwater fly rods are available for most budgets. Even a modestly priced model from a well-known maker will do the job. In some of the midpriced rods you can get the faster graphite and lighter blank weights that you get in the higher-priced units. Perhaps the most telling specification is the weight of the rod. The lighter the rod for a given line weight, the better. I would buy the lightest, fastest action—they will often go hand in hand—rod that I could afford that has an unconditional, lifetime warranty. These warranties are now almost standard, so don't be without one.

The other consideration is the number of pieces that your rod will come in. A two-piece rod has the best action and the least amount of weight, but two-piece rods cannot travel with you on most airline flights. If this is a

Figure 2.6 *Lifting power is greatly increased by using a lower rod angle. The more powerful butt section takes the pressure.*

consideration I'd go all the way to the four piece because even the three-piece units can't be carried on some airlines.

Reels

Like rods, serviceable reels are available for all budgets. Because the reels may last a long time I'd stick with one of the better known names, one with a history in the marketplace, so that parts will be available years down the road. You want a reel with a good disc drag system; some saltwater game fish can make substantial runs into the backing, and you'll need a good drag to wear down the fish.

Choose a reel's size based on the suggestion of the manufacturer. Start by picking the rod size that you will need for the kind of fishing you want to do. Most reel sizes are suggested for at least two line weights; I'd place a given size reel onto the largest weight rod that the manufacturer suggests. The reason is that the reel, and therefore the total outfit, will be lighter, and if you use Spectra backing material—more on this later—you'll have plenty of backing capacity. Also, given a choice of two similar reels, I'd choose the one with the larger spool diameter because it will retrieve line faster.

2.5 inches retrieves 7.85 inches per revolution

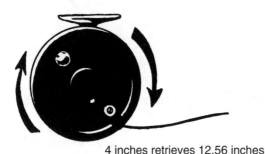

4 inches retrieves 12.56 inches per revolution

Figure 2.7 *The larger the reel diameter the greater the amount of line recovered per revolution.*

Most of today's reels are either cast and then painted, or machined and anodized. The latter is superior and not always much more expensive. Cast reels, though, are usually perfectly adequate. The larger the diameter of the spool, the faster the retrieve (see figure 2.7). The diameter changes as line is pulled from the reel, and therefore a wide-arbor reel will have a faster retrieve than a reel of less width because its diameter will remain larger as line is removed. Consider these reels if you can afford them and will be fishing for fish like the tunas that make long runs and then head back for the boat. Most fish, however, slug it out all the way back to the boat, and retrieve speed is not much of an issue.

The concept of antireverse has its advocates in saltwater fly fishing. By various mechanical means a strong pull against an antireverse reel will cause the line to pull out of the reel without the handle turning backward, as in the more common direct-drive reels. Some consider the direct-drive reels to be more positive because you are certain that line comes onto the reel when you turn the handle. I own both designs and am almost ambivalent for most uses. On my first trip fishing for false albacore I broke open the skin on the knuckles of my reel hand several times because of their astounding speed. I was using a direct-drive reel, and although the jolt of the handle hitting my knuckles never was enough to break off a fish, it might have been. I've seen it happen to others. If I'm hooked to a very fast or strong fish, like a false albacore, big striper, or tarpon, I prefer an antireverse reel.

Lines

As in freshwater fishing the design of the line corresponds to the type of presentation that you will ask it to make. Because of the larger flies and greater distances involved, all saltwater lines use a weight-forward design. The exact architecture of the head, however, varies considerably, depending on whether the line is designed for stealth presentations, casting long distances, casting into the wind, or some other specialty. The array of choices is dizzying, and your chances for success in saltwater angling will not be materially enhanced by owning all of these specialty lines. For a few special applications within some fisheries a special line type may be a benefit, and we'll talk about these as we cover each individual fish. Saltwater fly fishers should, however, have a rudimentary selection of floating, intermediate, and sinking-tip lines. The best lines for many fishing situations are lines like the L.L. Bean Superheads or Orvis Depthcharge, which are 20- to 30-foot sinking heads, rated in grains of weight, permanently attached to a thinner running line.

One of the concepts that are found more frequently in saltwater than in freshwater is that of the changeable shooting head. A number of these lines are on the market today, including some where only the tip of the head is changed. The benefit of these lines is supposed to be that one line and several heads can meet a great variety of fishing situations; properly set up they can also cast a bit farther because you can use a finer diameter running line. The finer diameter lines, however, have their problems, especially tangling.

I've spent a lot of time with shooting-head lines and have made up many custom designs. As a tackle tinkerer I enjoy dreaming up some new combination of head and running line that I hope will be more effective in some particular application. In the end, however, I usually end up going back to the one-piece, factory-made lines. The reason for this is the connection between the head and running line. Invariably this connection is clunky going in and out of the guides, weakens more quickly than the rest of the line, and creates a hinge point that makes casting unpleasant. I'd suggest that you stay away from changeable head lines.

The greatest enemy of all fly lines is dirt of any type. Lines get dirty from contact with everything. It's unavoidable. By taking the time to clean your lines with a quality line dressing after every trip into the salt, they'll perform much better.

The other big problem with fly lines is line twist. This problem isn't as obvious in freshwater because one seldom uses as much line as in the ocean. When you make long casts with a line that has a thinner diameter running line, the twists that are inevitable in fly casting will migrate down to the running line and cause some maddening tangles. Keeping your line clean and lubricated will help, but unless you enjoy fishing while angry you need to troll it behind a boat or twirl the head and some of the running line in the air in a direction that will untwist it.

In any case, you'll need a way to change lines quickly, unless you plan to buy and carry with you a reel for every fly line. In a few pages we'll show you a good system.

Backing

Backing material is of two basic types: Dacron and Spectra. The differences sum up simply. Dacron is almost twice as thick per pound test, has more stretch, costs less, and is easier to tie effective knots in—though not much. I've switched everything for saltwater over to Spectra. You retain a much faster rate of retrieve should a big fish run you well into your backing because the spool diameter doesn't change nearly as quickly. Spectra is also more abrasion resistant. Because most fly reels don't come with specifications for their backing capacity, when using Spectra you first may need to wind on the fly line that you plan to use—use a floating line to be a bit conservative—and then the backing. You'll have to use another reel to take it all back off, and then you'll have to wind the backing back on, but you'll have just the right amount of backing on the reel.

Flies

The most glaring differences between freshwater and saltwater flies are that virtually all saltwater flies are made to mimic some kind of baitfish, rather than an insect, and that saltwater flies are on the whole larger. We'll offer suggestions on flies for each subject species. I also suggest that you contact local fly shops for the best flies in a given area and for any particular species of game fish, including many that aren't covered in this book. An observation shared by many experienced guides is that too many anglers think that one fly or another is magic. Rather than concentrating on the far more important presentation or retrieve, some anglers will quickly lose faith in a fly and waste time looking through their flies for that nonexistent magical pattern. Unless you enjoy collecting flies—as some do—save your money and stay with a good selection of the basic, proven patterns.

Another observation on saltwater flies and fly tying is that synthetic materials are taking over. Only in a few of my larger deceiver patterns, in which I still prefer bucktail and saddle hackles to synthetics, do I use many natural materials. You must, of course, use rust-proof hooks—stainless hooks are hard to beat—or your flies will become useless.

For the safety of you and the fish, mash the hook's barb flat with a pair of pliers.

Other Equipment and Accessories

A few items will make your life in saltwater more efficient and pleasurable.

• **Stripping basket.** Although most freshwater fly fishers don't use a stripping basket, they are nearly indispensable in the salt, especially if there is any wave action. Although many types are on the market, I like the kind that looks like a dishpan, and that's exactly what some of them started as (see figure 2.8). These devices fasten around the waist with a belt and hold the line as you strip it in. The drawbacks to baskets are that you can't run a boat with one on or comfortably perform the single-handed strip—especially a

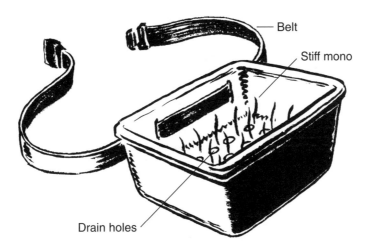

Figure 2.8   Saltwater shore anglers really need a good stripping basket.

Figure 2.9   A saltwater fly fisher using a stripping basket.

long one, which has its applications. If you hold your hands above the basket, tuck your rod under your arm, and retrieve hand over hand, the line should drop neatly in the basket, out of the way of both your feet and the surf's wave action (see figure 2.9).

• **Lights.** A great deal of saltwater fly fishing is done in low-light conditions. A number of excellent small lights are on the market. I have found the simplest and most satisfactory type to be a small plastic mini-flashlight, which I keep hung around my neck with an old piece of fly line. I often hold the light in my teeth so I can point it where necessary without using my hands.

• **Tools.** Always carry a small file and a pair of pliers. Sharpen hooks on the outside of the point, then deburr the inside so that they'll stick when dragged gently over a fingernail (see figure 2.10). Long-nosed pliers with a cutter blade can quickly cut a hook off at the bend, nip a fly from a heavy leader, or pull a fly out of a toothy fish's mouth.

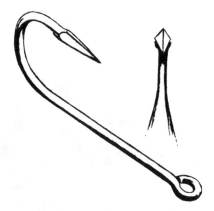

Figure 2.10 *Hooks sharpened on the outside of the point catch better than those sharpened on the inside, which tend to cut, not penetrate.*

Equipment Care and Storage

Freshwater fly fishing has its hallmark vest. Although you can wear a vest in the saltwater, most anglers choose not to. In the boat, I work directly from a tackle bag. There are many types of bags, but whatever you choose should be waterproof. Saltwater will destroy everything—including the bag—given the chance. Inside the bag you can carry your flies in clear, compartmentalized, plastic boxes, like the one shown in figure 2.11, as well as other equipment, such as spare reel spools, leader and tippet material, dry paper towels

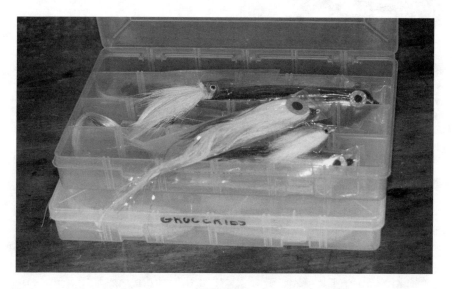

Figure 2.11 *Storing your flies in large, waterproof, dividable plastic boxes is a good way to organize them.*

Figure 2.12 *A chest pack keeps your flies, pliers, file, tippet material, and other equipment out of the saltwater while you're wading.*

and glasses cleaner, binoculars, a hand-held GPS, an all-in-one tool like the Leatherman, fly-line cleaner, lip balm, and sunscreen.

While wading some form of chest pack is functional (see figure 2.12). Chest packs go from ultraskimpy to quite large. I prefer something of modest size that won't be in my way. Inside the chest pack I like to keep my flies in fleece wallets—one or two at most should do it. I also carry made-up leaders and tippets in clear plastic envelopes along with a pair of pliers and a file—kept around your waist in a sheath they'll get wet when wading. Pay no attention to fly storage patches, especially exposed ones—you're guaranteed to lose your flies.

I store all my fly lines on the Rio Line Winder system, shown in figure 2.13. I use braided mono—more on this later—loop-to-loop connections on my fly lines and backing so that I can quickly change whole fly lines, leaders, or tippets. Mark the end of your lines that connect to the backing with a water-proof marker. Draw a thick circle for every five line weights and a thin one for each additional (figure 2.14). When you pick up the end of the line to

Figure 2.13 *Fly lines stored on Rio spools can be quickly looped-to-looped to your backing for an in-the-field line change.*

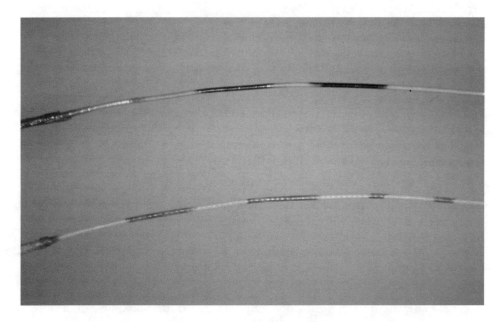

Figure 2.14 *The line on top is a 10-weight; the one on the bottom is a 12-weight—two long marks and two short ones.*

connect to the backing you'll know if it's the correct weight. You can also write not only the weight of line but also the type of line—sinking, floating, and so on—onto the Rio spool with the marker. I take extra lines, already set up, with me by storing their Rio spools in a plastic index-card box that stays in my tackle bag.

I wash my rods and reels with soap and water after every trip into the salt; flies should receive the same treatment. At least annually I go over the exterior of my reels and the rod guides with an old toothbrush and WD-40, and I wax the rod blanks with automotive wax. I pull the spools off the reels and oil them with a reel oil wherever I see an opening. Since I'm not much of a mechanic, if that doesn't keep them running properly they go back to the factory. I have a number of saltwater fly reels that have delivered years of flawless performance under this simple maintenance regimen.

Bench Work (Knots and Connections)

Most saltwater fish that get away do so not by breaking rods or fly lines; instead the connections or leaders let go. Sound backing-to-flyline and flyline-to-leader connections—and ones that pass easily through the guides—are vital.

Braided mono is the best material for making most of the connections needed to rig a saltwater fly-fishing outfit. I'm more than satisfied with this material—its ease of use, its durability, and the smoothness of its connections. Braided mono is available in 100-foot spools, and it's easy to make all your connections with this material. Use 30-pound test for lines up to 10-weight and 40- or 50-pound test for lines 10-weight and up. Here's how to use it to attach leaders to lines and lines to backing.

Butt Leaders and Backing Loops

A butt leader is an attachment to the end of your fly line in which you usually tie a loop so that you can simply attach leaders loop to loop.

Slide the braided mono onto the end of your fly line—you may need to unravel a bit of the end to start it. Using the inch-worm technique work the braid about 2 inches onto the fly line. Trim off the unwoven strands to leave a neat end; cut the braid off, leaving about 18 inches hanging beyond the end of the fly line, as shown in figure 2.15. Thread the tip of the braid through the end of a large sewing or craft needle. Select a point on the braided mono about 5 inches from the end and stick the needlepoint through the wall of the braid. Inch the needle along through the core of the braid for about 2 inches, in the direction of the fly line. Then pull it out through the wall of the braid, bringing the tip of the braid with it. Stretch the connection and trim off any excess (figure 2.16). You should end up with a 1-inch loop to connect leaders

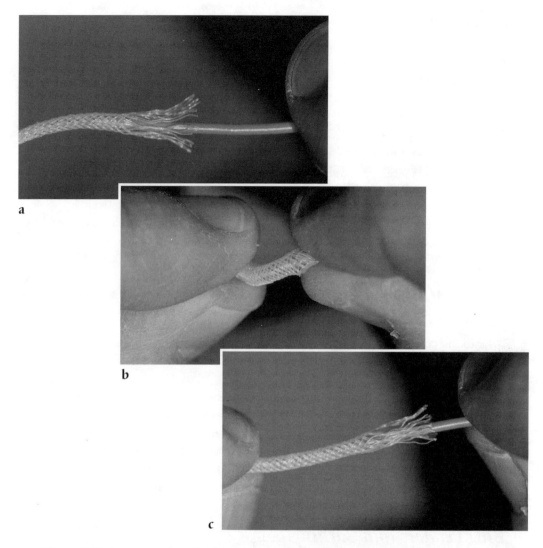

Figure 2.15 *Sequence a, b, and c shows how to insert a fly line into braided mono.*

to, about 12 inches of braided material, and 2 inches of braid over the tip of the fly line. Use two coats of a rubbery cement called Pliobond to secure the braid to the line and the braid threaded through the core to itself. See figure 2.17. No knots are needed, the glue will penetrate through the pores of the braid and hold strongly, the second coat will make everything smooth, and the rubbery nature of the Pliobond will leave the whole thing flexible. Make an identical loop on the other end of your fly line to attach the backing to. Note that some spools of the braided mono have a waxy material on them that comes off like dandruff when you handle the line. Cut off a length of this braid, wash it in soap and hot water, and allow it to dry before using it.

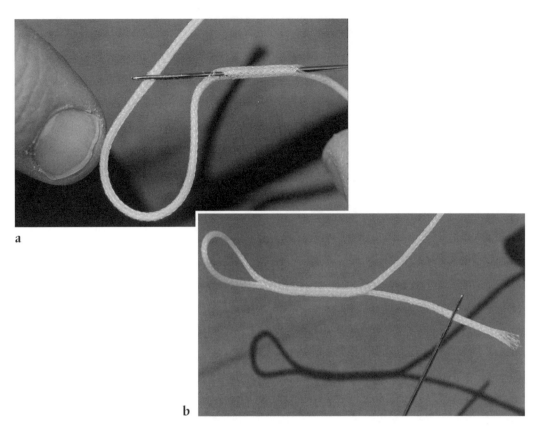

a

b

Figure 2.16 *Sequence a and b shows how to make a loop in braided mono.*

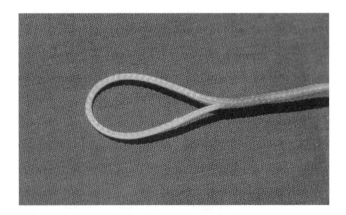

Figure 2.17 *Here is the finished loop created in figure 2.16. The area where the braid passes through itself is treated with two coats of Pliobond. It won't fail.*

Thread the fly-line end of your backing material into a needle and run it up through the core of some braided mono for about two inches; pull the needle and backing out through the braid. With the tag end of the backing tie a nail knot around the outside of the braid where the backing emerges from the braid. Trim any unwoven ends of braid and coat the nail knot and braid, back to where the backing goes in, with two coats of Pliobond, as shown in figure 2.18. You may need a little extra Pliobond to fill the area where the backing enters the braid.

Now, in the braid that you just attached to the backing, make a loop just like the one at the end of your butt leader, but make it at least six inches long.

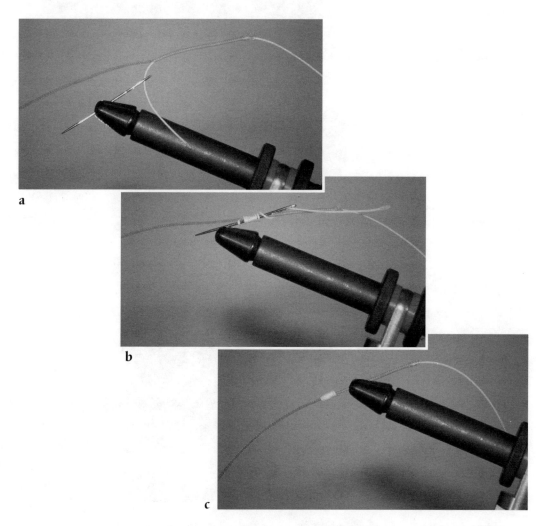

Figure 2.18 *Sequence a, b, and c shows how to connect flyline backing to a braided mono loop. This loop is used for loop-to-loop connections to the flyline.*

This long loop allows you to pass it around a reel or a Rio Line Winder box so that you can connect and disconnect complete fly lines using the loop-to-loop method (see figure 2.19). I've tried several methods, and this is the best combination I've found of a strong, smooth, and convenient way to attach the line to the backing.

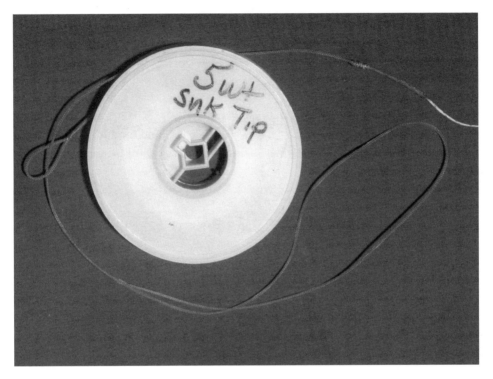

Figure 2.19 *Simply pass the loop in the backing through the loop in the end of the fly line, then pass the whole spool through the large loop.*

Knots and Leaders

This section combines knots and leaders because with the use of braided mono the only knots other than a nail knot that you'll have to learn are the ones used in making leaders and attaching flies.

You can fish for most of our subject fish except tarpon, the only big game fish listed here, with one simple tapered, nine-foot leader (figure 2.20).

Start with five feet of 30-pound test. Tie a small double surgeon's loop in one end (see figure 2.21). To the other end, using a double surgeon's knot, attach a two-and-one-half-foot length of 20-pound test.

In the 20-pound test tie a one-inch double surgeon's loop; attach the tippet to this by loop to loop. The tippet should start as a three-foot section of the

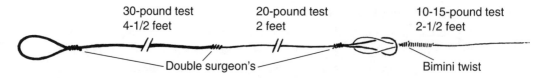

30-pound test   20-pound test   10-15-pound test
4-1/2 feet   2 feet   2-1/2 feet

Double surgeon's   Bimini twist

Figure 2.20 *A simple saltwater leader for most situations.*

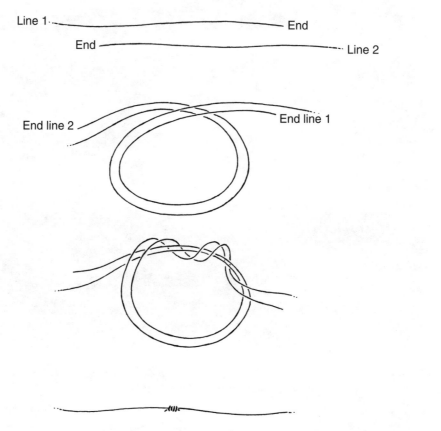

Line 1 ⋯⋯⋯⋯⋯⋯⋯⋯⋯⋯⋯⋯⋯⋯⋯ End

End ⋯⋯⋯⋯⋯⋯⋯⋯⋯⋯⋯⋯⋯ Line 2

End line 2   End line 1

Figure 2.21 *The double surgeon's connection. Use the folded-over end of one line only to make a double surgeon's loop.*

desired pound test, in which you tie a small, one-inch-loop Bimini twist, as shown in figure 2.22.

Less all the material used in tying knots, this leader should end up around nine feet long. Changing flies and abrasion from toothy fish will cause you to use up tippets; the Bimini twist loop will retain high breaking strength even in lighter pound tests. You can quickly and easily attach fresh tippets, which you carry with you pre-tied with the small Biminis, using the loop-to-loop method.

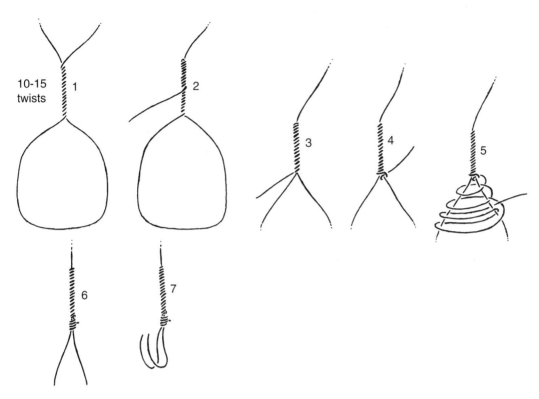

Figure 2.22 *The Bimini twist is the strongest possible knot with which to make a loop or doubled line.*

For tarpon, tie a double surgeon's loop in each end of four feet of 30-pound test; loop to loop this onto your butt leader (see figure 2.23). Next, construct a class tippet by tying a Bimini twist, with an extra long loop, in each end of a piece of the desired pound-test mono; the class tippet should be 18 inches long not counting the knots. The loop on one end is doubled over and tied into a double-strand loop by using a double surgeon's knot; this end attaches loop to loop to the 30-pound test you added to your butt leader. On the other end of the class tippet, cut the Bimini loop to form two equal single strands; this end attaches to the bite tippet. Because of the raspy mouths of these fish,

Figure 2.23 *The tarpon leader features 100 percent breaking strength biminis and an 80- to 100-pound-test shock tippet.*

tarpon flies are attached, often by snelling the hook, to an 80- or 100-pound-test bite tippet. Attach the class tippet permanently with a Huffanagle or an Albright knot to the bite tippet (see figure 2.24). Store the fly, bite tippet, and class tippet on a stretcher to keep the heavy line straight and change as a unit. I'm not spending much time on this because if you decide to fish for tarpon you'll undoubtedly start with a guide, or at least an experienced friend, and use their specialized equipment to introduce you to this fishing.

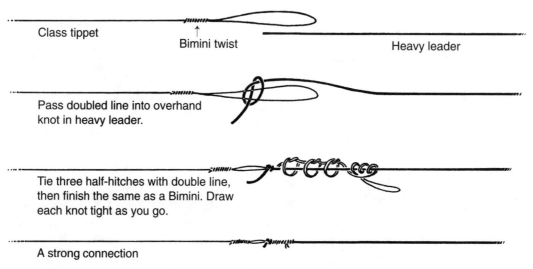

Figure 2.24 *To tie the Huffanagle knot, first make a double line in the end of your class tippet material with a Bimini twist.*

Many satisfactory knots are available to connect flies to leaders. The duncan loop, however, and a modification of it that creates a noncollapsible loop for the fly to swim from will do the job for almost all saltwater fly fishing. Figure 2.25 shows the duncan loop.

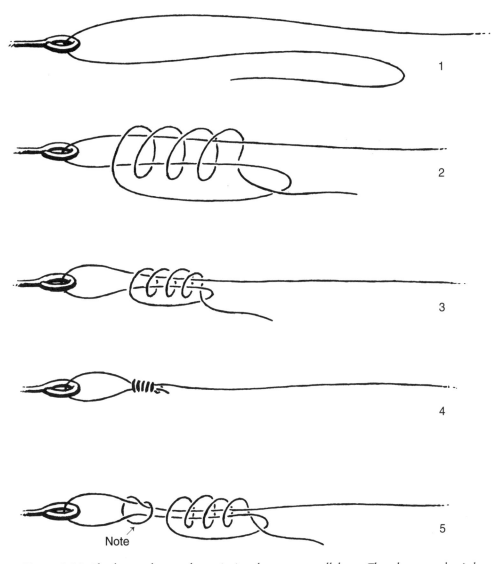

1

2

3

4

5

Note

Figure 2.25 *The duncan loop and a variation that cannot pull down. These knots can be tied—with a lot of practice—with your eyes shut.*

Chapter

3

Finding, Presenting to, and Handling Fish

Bits of Wisdom

Although a great deal of angling is blind casting to likely structures, most of the species that we'll be discussing are occasionally visible to the angler. They may be clearly visible, such as a bonefish swimming on a shallow sand flat, or they may become visible breaking the surface of the water while chasing prey. Some species, like bonito, are rarely caught by fly rodders unless they first give themselves away by surface feeding. I've caught many of them, however, by searching the area where they had recently surfaced for the slightest signal about where they might have gone and then blind casting in that direction. Even when a fish is clearly visible it may not immediately draw your attention. Here are a few things that may help you locate fish visually.

Detecting Fish

The side effects of feeding activity frequently give away the location of fish. The presence of a school of stripers is often indicated by a lone gull stationed on a point nearby. Terns many times dive over surfacing bonito and false albacore, hoping to seize the tiny baitfish rushing to the surface to escape the predators. Look for shorebirds sitting on the water, positioned on strategic pieces of shorefront, or darting toward the water from the air. One foggy day in Maine, a guide friend of mine located a school of feeding stripers by heading in the direction from which terns were flying with small herring still flopping in their bills.

Not all visual giveaways are birds. Predators may appear as dark shadows under the water, sometimes initially visible only by the black pupils of their eyes. In the shallows you may often see the wake of a swimming fish or its flash as it turns on its side to feed. The shiny sides reflect in the sun; some call this mooning. On other days the torn bodies of oily baitfish savaged by toothy predators will allow enough oil to drift to the surface to form a slick or smooth spot on the water's surface. On the flats, fish are sometimes given away by the muddy or silty spot that they create while grubbing in the bottom for crabs or worms. Often you can hear the pop of fish feeding on the surface; if you hear the sound but don't see the fish, look into the wind. The sound of feeding fish carries well with the wind, but they must be very close for the sound to go upwind. Often you can even catch the scent of fish carried on the wind. You can easily smell oily baitfish, like herring, if they are in shallow water. Be observant on the water; use your senses. If you can locate the fish to cast to, you're halfway there.

Approaching the Fish

Once you locate the fish, you must make your approach. Even if a guide is silently poling you toward your target, it's important to be quiet and keep your silhouette low. Fish learn early in life that trouble can come from the air. I've seen tightly packed schools of fish jump in panic as a cloud's shadow passed over the water. If you're on your own and need to motor over to a school of fish that is breaking on the surface, don't despair. The motor does not always scare fish. Saltwater fish are accustomed to motors from the commercial fishers who work around them, sometimes constantly. What troubles them the most is a high-winding motor running directly over them. I usually approach surface-feeding fish at a moderate speed, pull up within casting distance, and leave the motor idling while I make my first cast. I learned while chasing cruising brook trout—fish that were moving along and rising sporadically to feed on insects—that the constant sound of the motor doesn't always bother fish greatly, but turning it on and off does. On the other hand, if you can position yourself uptide or upwind of fish that are still likely to be there when you arrive, you can drift silently into position. Whenever you approach breaking fish, time may be of the essence.

Casting and Retrieving

When making your cast, try not to beat the water if you know you are casting to a fish. The water haul that we discussed earlier is a good technique but not under delicate circumstances. Make your cast to the fish from as far away as you can make an accurate presentation. If you are casting to a school, don't just plunk the fly down in the middle of the whole group, especially if they are in shallow water or it is very calm. The line or the fly, either in the air or as they touch the water, can spook the school. Cast to the edges of the school, preferably to the front edge if they're moving because that's where the largest fish are likely to be. Strive to make your presentation natural. Baitfish will swim away from predators, not toward them; your fly should do the same.

You should style your retrieve to accomplish a type of baitfish behavior. In some cases a realistic fly may be dead drifted in the water to mimic a baitfish injured by a previous predator and now vulnerable. Often, a fly cannot be stripped fast enough to imitate a large, panicked baitfish trying to escape a predator that it has just seen. Long arm movements give the impression of great speed. The pauses between strips, especially if random, may further suggest panic, injury, and vulnerability. Unless you are constantly drawing strikes, try varying your retrieve. Use both the conventional single-hand strip and the hand-over-hand, or two-handed, retrieve shown in figure 3.1, which can yield a seductive swimming action as the rod tip springs back and forth with the rhythm of the hand-over-hand motion.

When a fish takes the fly you must set the hook. Some fish, like tarpon, have bony, tough mouths and require that you pull rapidly on the line while deeply bending the rod; straight lining the fish is likely to break the tippet.

Figure 3.1   *The two-handed retrieve can set up vibrations that produce a seductive swimming action in the fly.*

Often, though, the need to set the hook hard is overstated. If your hook is sharp—and it should be like a razor—a solid tug is all that you'll need.

Many freshwater anglers have never had a fish make it to the reel, never mind into the backing. If your equipment is realistically sized for the fish you are after, you will have more than enough backing. I like to set a fairly firm drag at around 25 percent of the breaking strength of the tippet—you will usually guess on the low side—and palm the reel for more tension. Keep the rod fairly low, which applies pressure to the butt instead of the tip. Most rods are broken on big fish as they near the boat by anglers who stand at the gunwale and pull the rod way over backward, severely overloading the tip and the ferrule. Move back away from the gunwale so that your guide can handle the fish. Leave at least one full rod length of line hanging out of the tip to give the guide some room to work. If you reel the fish right to the rod tip, neither you nor the guide can get at it to unhook it.

If I'm handling a big fish alone, either from the boat or while wading, I pull some slack from the reel, hold the rod and line with one hand near the middle of the rod, and point the tip at the fish. Then I position the fingers of my other hand into a ring, which I slide down the rod until I can grab the line. I then release the slack line held in reserve, and now I am hand lining the fish. If the critter regains its vigor, I can release the slack and let it swim off. Then I can put it back on the rod and try again. See figure 3.2.

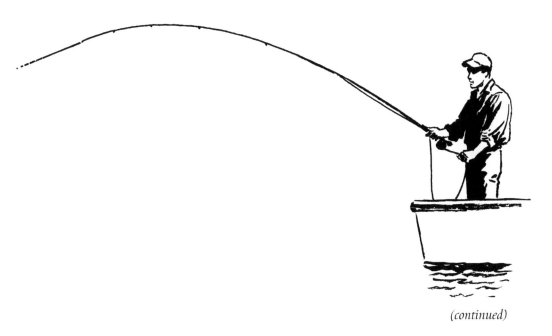

(continued)

Figure 3.2   *This sequence shows how to land a big fish either while in a boat or while wading without breaking your rod.*

Figure 3.2 *(continued)*

Many saltwater game fish are simply too large to lift into the boat, and some have teeth that prohibit you from putting your hand near their mouths. If you're a purist about things you can probably tail all but the largest of these fish. Grab the tired fish firmly by the narrow part of the body that's just in front of the tail fin. Very large tarpon, snook, redfish, and stripers can be handled by the mouth with the protection of gloves. Another method, especially if you are wearing gloves, is simply to grab the tired fish by the back of

Figure 3.2 *(continued)*

the head and hold it while removing the hook. Gloves will allow a secure hold without crushing the fish; wet them to minimize the removal of the fish's protective slime. Some species have sharp fins, gill plates, or teeth, but if you grab the fish securely behind the head you're safe. Unless you plan to eat these fish, it's best to leave them right in the water while unhooking them. Studies have shown that the length of time that fish are held out of the water is the most critical element in their survival. I find that if I apply sufficient pressure during the fight, either a very short recovery time or none at all is necessary before release. Used properly the fly rod exacts a very low mortality during catch-and-release fishing.

Travel Angling

To me, travel angling is any angling outside my home waters. Depending on where you are as you read this book, one or more of the subject species and locations may be right in your backyard. That fishery may be two thousand miles from another reader, who has another of our selections in their own home waters. By design, however, every world-class fishery that we discuss here is in the continental United States; most readers will find several within a one-day drive. What's the allure to travel angling? Why go half a continent away, or drive even five hours, just to catch the fish in someone else's backyard?

I once had a fishing friend out on Maine's Kennebec River. The man had been privileged to fish and hunt all over the world. At one point this gentleman had a seagoing sportfishing boat, complete with captain, and moved it constantly around the Caribbean and the Gulf of Mexico in search of billfish. Toward the end of our second day on the water my friend connected with a 30-pound striped bass that put up a glorious resistance on a 10-weight fly rod. As the large bass finally popped into view at boatside, the normally reserved man, now as gleeful as a child, bubbled out loud to himself, "Now this is what I came here for."

I watched him unhook the fish, step back, look around appreciatively, and bask in the moment. Maine's rugged shoreline, the turbulent tide rips of the Kennebec, and this excellent bass became another valuable memory in a lifetime of exceptional fishing.

Each of the fisheries that we're about to discuss offers something different—the brawling style of the striper, the waters of the Jersey shore and Montauk Point, the pandemonium of an acre of thrashing false albacore, a school of redfish tailing in a sweltering Texas backwater, the eye-popping spectacle of a six-foot tarpon greyhounding through a Marquesas sunrise. I've seen these things and wouldn't trade them for all of Wall Street's millions—unless that meant I'd be able to experience them more often.

For the angler, this book is a kind of home-shopping program. You may be happy just to read about these superb fish and how to catch them. But you may also wish to try them yourself. We have you both in mind as we write this. We hope this information will give you an idea about which fish to go after, about which places and species capture your imagination. But no matter which that may be, or even what other travel angling destinations you may select, the information we're about to provide can help you achieve the highest level of satisfaction from your fishing excursion.

A Chat With Chip

My friend Chip Bates, owner of Angler Adventures, makes his living by making sure that people have a good time on trips to places like Patagonia, Alaska, Andros Island, and Labrador. Chip is an excellent angler, one of the best and most modest fly casters to get on my boat. As I once heard Lefty Kreh say about another fly caster, "The man can cast a fly line through a screen door." So Chip knows fly fishing and understands what it takes for the visiting angler to have a good trip. I spent a morning picking Chip's brain on what to do and what to look out for in travel angling. Here are some of the things we discussed.

The toughest customers to please are the ones who equate what they spend on the trip with how good the fishing is. Much of the price of a fishing trip, especially to a remote location, is the cost to run the physical plant of the lodge. The task is daunting. There are meals to prepare—the more you pay, the fancier those should be—guides to manage, equipment to maintain, and on and on. All of this has nothing to do with how good the fishing is. But you can access virtually all the destinations that we'll be discussing for relatively modest expense, with the possible exception of a guide. Nonetheless, fishing at many of these continental U.S. locations is among the best in the world.

The best-laid fishing plans mean little if the weather turns bad. Some places and some fisheries, especially at certain times of the year, are far more influenced by the weather than others. You must understand this. If you can't fish because of the weather, then you simply can't fish—it may not be safe. Taking chances in rough water or trying to make your guide do it will only make things worse. If it's possible to get a last-minute forecast before your final commitment to a fishing trip, then you're blessed.

Your guide can make or break your trip. If the lodge or outfitter that you are booking through works by assigning specific guides in advance, make sure that you receive written confirmation of who your guide will be and which days you will be fishing with him. If possible use a guide recommended by someone you know and trust. Expect to pay a deposit to most guides to reserve your days on the water. My experience, and Chip's, has been that many guides are loose with their records. The ones who aren't organized enough to be concerned about things like deposits and reserved days probably aren't as concerned as they should be about other aspects of their job. Make sure that you iron out a few things first such as what kind of boat you will be using, whether it is set up for fly rods, who supplies lunch and drinks, what time and where you meet the guide, and whether the guide supplies adequate fly-fishing equipment or whether you should bring your own. Is the equipment that the guide will provide right-hand or left-hand retrieve? I always like to use my

(continued)

43

A Chat With Chip (continued)

own equipment, but sometimes that may be impossible, such as a spur-of-the-moment decision to add fishing to a business trip.

Chip also warned that all good fishing destinations are more heavily fished than in the past. The further in advance you can plan, the better. I would add that although you can book any of the destinations in this book yourself, the services of an agency like Chip's are usually included in a lodge's or even a guide's rates, and an agency has expertise in making their trips run smoothly.

Chip sent me a number of checklists that accompany his various destinations. We covered virtually all the necessary equipment in the last chapter but you could add an alligator clip and lanyard to hold your hat so it won't blow off your head, a repair kit for your glasses, and a first-aid kit. Even though I think that we've got it covered, a checklist from a local tackle shop or your guide is a good idea.

Clothing

Proper clothing is important to the enjoyment of any angling trip. The first consideration is where you will store it. Whenever I step onto a boat for any more than a few minutes of fishing in sight of the dock, I carry a waterproof duffel bag. Several types of these bags are available. I have no special preferences except to dislike the ones shaped like a skinny tube. How can you find anything unless it's right on top?

Fishing throughout most of the United States often exposes you to a significant range of temperatures during the day. Morning is likely to be the coldest, and you must consider the speed of the boat in the damp air. Everything on the boat is likely to be wet with dew. Later in the day, during almost any month when you might engage in the fisheries in this book, it may become hot as blazes. And it can rain at any time, or the boat ride can soak you with spray.

The answer is to layer with modern, lightweight, breathable synthetics. A fleece bottom and top and a fleece neck gaiter under a breathable foul-weather suit with hood will keep you warm and dry even on an October morning at Montauk. Later on everything goes in the bag, and out comes sunblock and a flats-type hat. For the ride in, if it has breezed up, you can put on part or all of the foul-weather stuff. I also suggest a short pair of rubber boots. In New England I wear them all day long, but elsewhere I exchange them for sneakers later in the day. Some like to go barefoot; they claim that they can tell if they're standing on the line. Maybe so, but I'm just not comfortable walking around a fishing boat in bare feet. It may seem a bit much, but I've also gone to wearing a pair of CO_2 inflatable suspenders just in case.

You probably won't even notice them, and they could save your life, especially if you're alone.

Trip Planning

If you'll be spending all your time with a guide this won't be quite as relevant. If, however, you plan to go off on your own, or if you're going to be doing some wade fishing and would like to move around the area, then a little forethought can add much to your trip. I split most of my saltwater time between Maine and Cape Cod, but the cape is for me the newer area, the frontier. I spend some winter hours looking at charts, trying to find attractive areas that have escaped my scrutiny. Once I choose a new area or technique to try I plan an approach to it. If I'm going to a new fishing area, I'll buy a chart of the waters I plan to fish and read everything I can find about the fishing I plan to do. During the months leading up to my trip I try to contact people who have already fished this area, and I make a checklist of equipment. When the time draws near packing is easy. Over the years I've arrived better prepared than most and been able to get the most out of my trips.

When it comes down to the day of fishing the same planning applies. Almost 30 years ago I spent fall weekends with my fishing partner Phil Perrino on the island of Martha's Vineyard. We were young and fished from dusk to dawn, then slept a few hours in the back of my truck before doing some four-wheel-drive reconnaissance along the island's beaches. We analyzed the wind, tides, presence of baitfish, and reports from our fellow anglers. From this information we often created a written plan—usually on the back of an old Dunkin' Donuts bag—for the evening's fishing. Our plans often took us on an after-dark, whirlwind tour of the island, shifting from place to place with different phases of the tide or directions of wind, and from time to time we caught a lot of large striped bass. Sometimes it was just determination to stick to our plan that pushed us wearily late at night; then suddenly we walked onto a beach full of action. Without an advance plan we'd never have fared as well.

PART II

Favorite Fish and Fishing Destinations

A FEW YEARS BACK I SPENT A LOT OF TIME FISHING WITH MY FRIEND AND MENTOR BROCK APFEL. Brock ran L.L. Bean's fly-fishing department, but in an earlier life he'd been an executive in the oil industry and had lived and fished in several parts of the world. Here are two of the most memorable things he ever told me.

Brock and his wife, Joan, were living in Libya when Khadafi came to power. "What was that like?" I asked him, expecting a tale of terror about someone who has become one of the world's most notorious madmen.

"Not so bad," said Brock. "The country needed a strong leader. He did some positive things and was really quite popular."

I mention this only to demonstrate that Brock is quite flexible in the way he looks at things.

Brock has since moved to Florida, where he's specialized in fishing the remote recesses of a large, nearby bay system. Brock uniquely planned his approach to the area by deciding to limit his fishing to a few square miles of some inaccessible backcountry.

"I've even gone to carrying a GPS," said Brock.

"Wow," I said. "Is it that hard to find your way back into there?"

"Oh no," Brock replied. "I've learned every twist and turn. I carry the GPS so that in case I break down, I can explain to someone where I am!"

Another time I asked Brock, "Of all the fishing you've done, and in all the places you've done it, what do you like the best?"

"More and more," said Brock thoughtfully, "the fishing I like the best is the fishing that's just outside my back door."

So maybe it's appropriate that we start our list of saltwater fly fishing's finest fish and destinations with one that's just outside our back door. I'm from Maine, and John's adopted it, or perhaps it's adopted him. So it's easy for us to see Maine's rugged, spectacular coast as a great destination. What I find interesting to think of, though, is how many fine places there are, and how passionate many of the local fishers are about them and the fishing they provide. And all these great places, and great fisheries, are just outside somebody's back door.

Chapter
4

Striped Bass— Kennebec River, Maine

A river that once held more fish in every cubic foot of its lively waters than any other in the nation, Maine's Kennebec has long been a river of legends. Many are true, and if some are not wholly factual, they spring from this river's rich realities.

It was on the Kennebec that a few English colonists built the first settlement in what was to become, more than a century later, the United States of America. That first year, those settlers survived on the Kennebec's fish and shellfish. Of those fish, the striped bass was among the most plentiful.

This is a muscular river of swift tides and remarkable resilience, a river that has survived a century of abuse and lived to regain much of its identity as a river of fish. Like the Kennebec, the striped bass has demonstrated an indomitable will to live, fighting not only for its survival but for the dominant place it once held among the Northeast's finest game fish.

The combination of the two—this heavyweight of a tidal river and this formidable fish—is an angler's dream come true, a dream even more compelling for those who cast flies. The Kennebec holds every kind of water— mud-flat shallows that are the Yankee version of the subtropical flats that stretch from south Florida beyond the Bahamas; riffling stretches of white water that dash along bouldered bottoms as prettily as any Adirondack trout stream; quiet backwaters where gentle eddies maintain a kind of static equi-librium, a pond held fast in the river's embrace; rushing torrents compressed between twin granite cliffs, torrents deep enough to float great, gray ships of war with room to spare beneath their keels; marshes rich with wild rice and stiff with bulrushes where hidden channels quiver as silver baitfish are chased from the depths; and the river's broad, tide-torn delta where the Kennebec meets the Atlantic, where boulders are dashed by great waves, and where currents are too turbulent to be trusted. Here the ocean's constant swells tell you these are unforgiving waters, even though they are embraced by the two arms of clear sand beach where the greatest stripers assemble and lie like logs, gleaming emerald above the pale Atlantic floor.

All these, and more, are the Kennebec, a river of infinite angling possibili-ties, a river that gathers lesser tributaries into its embrace, a river embroi-dered with a thousand tidal streams and floods of silver schooling fish. An angler can fish the Kennebec for three lifetimes and still have more adven-tures waiting to be lived. With its depths etched in granite by great glaciers, its 10-foot tides, and its swirling masses of microorganisms that bloom when-ever the sun strikes the mud flats' dark fertility, the Kennebec is prolific beyond comprehension. Even now there are Kennebec shores that are as purely wild and natural as they were when Benedict Arnold led his flotilla of clumsy bateaux on that ill-fated expedition from Popham, where the Kennebec begins, to a distant Quebec. In those days before the river was dammed, the unwieldy boats must have floated above school after countless school of striped bass.

In the lower Kennebec, those schools have returned. They wait there for you, as they waited for me one Fourth of July dawn. With my friend Linwood at the helm of his small Whaler, we cruised downriver at half speed from Bowdoinham, parting the early morning mists as we crossed Merrymeeting Bay on our way to a rocky stretch of the Kennebec below Chops Point, a run of the river mottled with bouldered islands of stone spilled randomly by the glaciers that carved this river's course ten thousand years ago.

"Look there," Linwood said, raising his arm, pointing toward the east where clouds floated pink in the sunrise. We were greeted by a flight of eagles, seven of them, some juvenile, some adult, their white heads gleaming against the dusky plumage of broad wings. Like us, they were on a hunt, and, like ours, theirs would be blessed with the Kennebec's fecundity. Our boat was swept through the narrows at the Chops, where vast volumes of water are pinched between two stony points that almost touch, and we scuttled past Lines Island and then drifted in the current to the bouldered shallows that surround the confusion of Ram, Crawford, and Wood Islands.

Here we cast our flies—simple Lefty's deceivers on floating lines, for here the Kennebec becomes a mountain stream, babbling as it rushes along rocky bottoms with less than a foot to spare. Casting on an uptide quarter, we let the current sweep our flies past the shoals, on into the deeper cuts and gullies where stripers waited for the river to tumble such morsels their way. We had strikes on every fourth or fifth cast, small fish—two to four pounds— but these were the fish we expected. The Kennebec's heavyweights tend toward deeper gullies, darker places, and we were here for the joy of an early-morning Independence Day. As lively as any salmon or trout, charged with the abundant energy of their saltwater heritage, the young stripers taken in swift waters on light tackle were as challenging and entertaining as any fish that swims.

We were home before breakfast but brought with us memories that would last a lifetime. Now whenever I see an eagle, time takes me back to that dawn with Linwood and the Kennebec.

Thirty-five years later I fished close to the same waters, this time with Brad and Pat in Pat's considerably huskier boat. This was an October expedition, one of those bright, windy early autumn afternoons when the season's winey intoxication is its most dazzling—one of those days when the wind sweeps from the northwest and the air is charged with an elemental zest. We were off Thorne Island, in the lee of Line and well east of the water I'd shared with Linwood.

We had no trouble finding stripers. Running the boat a half mile up Burnt Jacket Channel along Thorne's easterly side, Pat shut down the motor and we spun broadside, drifting west with the current, the three of us casting all the way. Pat and Brad threw terminal line impregnated with lead to make certain their flies sank quickly into waters 25 to 40 feet down. I stayed with my floating line; I'd rather hook a single fish on the surface than 20 on one of those heavy lines.

That was about the ratio of my success to Pat's and Brad's. For in spite of the freshening northwester and the field of whitecaps that blossomed in its wake, striped bass were there by the thousands, schooled on the Thorne Island ledges, waiting there, noses into the tide, watching for tidbits tossed in the turbulence. Presented with yellow deceivers, the fish responded on al- most every cast. Most were 2- and 3-pounders, but every now and then a 10- or 12-pounder slammed the fly, and the anglers had to work for their fish.

As soon as a striper was boated and slipped from the barbless hook, it was weighed, tagged, and released. As officers of the Maine Chapter of the Coastal Conservation Association, Brad and Pat were doing their volunteer bit to help everyone discover just a bit more information about the striper's migra- tory movements. Some fish tagged in the Kennebec have been caught upriver within days; others have been taken off the New Jersey coast many miles south, some so soon after their Kennebec tagging that you have to wonder how a striper could have covered so much distance in such a short time.

As a kind of supercargo with no assigned duties, I had little to do but revel in the splendid effervescence of that autumn afternoon. Early October brings

Maine some of its finest days, and that was one of them. Under a dazzling sun, the windswept waters gleamed against a shore dappled with the yellow, orange, and crimson leaves of aspen, oak, and maple, each touched by the fall's first frosts. Toward evening, as we eased downriver to Bath, I knew the day would be my last on the river until spring. And I was sure that some of those stripers we tagged would be there waiting.

Waiting too would be their parents, grandparents, great-grandparents, and great-great-grandparents in schools of 30-, 40-, and 50-pound fish. Yes, 50-pounders, like those waiting for Brad and me on a soft, June dawn when pale mists lay like a coverlet on the Kennebec's currents. A flood tide had reached its peak, and the air was as still as stone. It was that magic fishing moment when the Kennebec's sheltered waters felt the ebb tide's first trembling, tentative tug. Throttling back as we neared Bluff Head, Brad turned his boat past Bluff Head Point where the Kennebec becomes a small bay of sheltered, shallow waters held in a curving arm of marsh grass cut by a winding, tidal stream. It is a cove always in the lee, one of the river's most placid places.

As we drifted east on the quiet water, as smooth as a pewter plate in the dawn's half light, I saw circular ripples wavering on the surface, ever widening rings, one set here, another there, and still another. Then a great, silver torso rolled, gleaming there in the mist, and a tail as wide as my two hands slapped the surface with a sharp crack that rattled my composure.

"Brad, Brad," I whispered, "these are all big fish. There's a whole school here. Look! There's another. We'll spook them if we're not careful. There isn't that much water here. Can't be more than six feet."

I needn't have babbled. Brad was already ahead of me. His 10-weight was in his hands. Stepping to the stern, he stripped line off the reel, made two powerful false casts, and sent one of his chicken-sized "grocery" flies sailing toward the spot where the last striped submarine had surfaced.

He retrieved quickly, forcefully, making the large fly behave like a fish in panic. Wham! The water boiled as if an anvil had fallen from the sky. But the line never tightened. The monster had missed its strike.

Not to worry. Even as Brad began a second cast, more huge fish splashed and rolled. We were drifting in a sea of heavyweights. My knees shook and my hands trembled as I tried to get my rod unlimbered.

"Fish on!" Brad shouted as his lines snapped taut, hissing, scattering silver droplets as his fish bulled across the shoals, full speed ahead for the deeper Kennebec waters off to the west. There went the fly line and a fast 100 yards of backing. The battle began. These were powerful fish, these 40- and 50-pound grown-ups, most of them with more than 20 years' experience with hooks, lines, and leaders. They knew how to fray a leader on a rock's hard edge, how to rub hooks free by scraping their jaws on a barnacled bottom. Just the sheer stubborn strength of their shaking heads had snapped scores of lines and leaders.

But Brad applied maximum pressure. Soon the fish knew it was beaten. Hoisted aboard, laid flat across the stern with a wet towel over its eyes to keep it immobile, the fish was measured, tagged, and the data noted for later entry into the records.

In less than a minute, the striper was back in the river as Brad gripped it just forward of its tail and eased the fish gently back and forth, helping it pump water through its gills. When he sensed its strength restored, Brad gave the fish an easy shove and let go, and we watched the 46-inch striper flex that impressive tail, shift into fast forward, and vanish.

In six minutes, the first evidence of the sun would rise over the trees and begin soaking up the morning's mist.

Brad favors the dawn. He is certain it is a favorite time for feeding stripers. It's an accurate observation, but there are few rules about when stripers will be hungry, especially in Kennebec territory.

One of the most spectacular striper dramas I can recall (and I shall never forget it) happened just after noon on a bright, cloudless day as the wind held gentle in the northwest, touching the sharp horizon with a fine clarity. We were aboard Vincent's 17-foot Whaler, then his newest possession. Proud at the helm, he and his wife, Tracy (our daughter), took me down the Kennebec from Bath, past the fort at Popham, past Bay Point, Stage Island, and Pond Island and on out onto the perpetually turbulent waters of Pond Island Shoal, the last shoal before the Seguin Ledges and Seguin itself mark the final landward outpost on the brink of the open Atlantic's heaving depths.

On that brilliant, hard-edged day, shimmering schools of silver-dollar-size herring flooded Pond Island Shoal as completely as any tide. They were everywhere, and everywhere they were chased by more multitudes of striped bass. Schools of 15- and 20-pounders surged across the sea's shining surface as terrified herring shot skyward—living fountains showering silver in the sunlight.

Drifting through fields of fish, we cast. Tracy and Vincent tossed bucktails from their spinning rods; when their fish were boated and released, I picked up my eight-weight and cast a large blue and white deceiver. One strip, two, and bang! I had a fish on, running line off the reel while all around us the spectacle continued. Terns, herring gulls, laughing gulls, great black backs circled, screaming, darting, and diving whenever white water marked a striper's surge and left crippled herring flailing in its wake. All the while we rose and fell on rolling swells born on a distant sea.

There are those fishing moments when adrenaline takes over, when pulse rates soar and every word is a shout. It has something to do with the unraveling violence that surrounds you, the unfettered wildness of so many thousands of powerful fish feeding in this single, small vortex of such a large and heaving sea. On that afternoon we were more than mere anglers; we became part of the frenzy.

In less than a half hour, the drama was over. Gulls dipped here and there, and then were gone. The sea's surface mirrored the high blue sky and appeared just as empty. If we had not happened on those waters precisely when we did, the Kennebec delta would have no sharers of its secret.

It is a river of many secrets.

Late September, and late in my fishing years, I discovered another. After lunch with Peter Cox at his home on Indian Point on the easternmost rim of the Kennebec's mouth, I picked up an eight-weight rod and walked over the point's monumental boulders rising there like the huge, rounded backs of great whales. At the water's edge, standing dry on the pebbles of a small beach, I cast into the quiet waters of the small cove at the entrance to Sagadahoc Bay.

The early autumn sun was high and bright; it was not a fishy day or time. But within 20 minutes I saw a riffle of darker blue on the cove's still surface. A moving school of baitfish of some sort, and beneath them . . . well, something was going on.

I made two casts in the general direction of the modest activity, then a third. A striped bass waited for that one and was at my feet in a few minutes, a four-pound fish gleaming there in the wash, brighter than any jewel. And I'd hardly wet my sneakers.

You'd need at least three lifetimes to discover most of the Kennebec's striper secrets. Even then, more surprises would be in store. It's that rich a river.

Tackle and Techniques

Since Colonial times the striped bass has been the most important sport fish north of Cape Hatteras. The striper can grow to over 100 pounds, and some over 60 pounds are caught along the coast every year. The stripers are creatures of shallow water, seldom found in depths of more than 100 feet, or more than a mile or so from the nearest land. Stripers often feed confidently at night in water that can barely cover their backs. The beginning angler, perched on a sod bank beside a tidal creek, with a baited rod propped up by a forked stick, catches them. They are also caught by the expert fly fisher, unleashing 100-foot casts at night over surf and currents from a turbulent inlet. Stripers forage the sand bottoms for crabs or worms, but I've seen large ones launch themselves clear of the water to catch a foot-long squid in mid-air. It is this versatility that causes men like Brock Apfel, once head of L.L. Bean's fly-fishing division and a man who has caught countless saltwater and freshwater game fish on a fly rod, to comment that the striper is among the most rewarding fish that can be taken on a fly rod.

Much of this versatility stems from the fish's classic design. Mitch Ryder sang, "She's not too skinny, but not too fat; a real humdinger, and I like it like that." I guess he was talking about a woman, but he might have been speaking of *Morone saxatilis*. The body of the striper is perhaps the most pleasing combination of design features of any fish in this book. This goes for more than their beautifully proportioned physical appearance. The muscles of the striper are a combination of the dark, red kind that characterizes tuna—fish designed for prolonged, high-speed, ocean swimming—and the white type that yields instant horsepower for short-burst pursuits. Additionally, the large eyes of the striper combine with a highly developed lateral line to make it as successful a predator in the dead of night as it is on a brightly lit, daytime flat. Decorated with large, streamlined fins and the prominent stripes of its namesake, the silvery green striped bass is as attractive to the eye as any fish.

Once on the line, the fight of the striper also reflects this versatility. Stripers can hang down on their sides like powerful jacks, they can peel 100 yards of backing from a reel with a stiff drag, and when hooked in the shallows even the big ones can put some air between themselves and the water. Stripers lack sharp teeth, and if the hook holds and the fish finds no rocks to wrap around, you should have a good chance of landing even the larger individuals.

Nearly all the striped bass on the East Coast come from either Chesapeake Bay or the Hudson River, most from the Chesapeake. Relatively fecund, a big female bass spawns millions of eggs into her natal waters. If survival is good, most of these young stripers, upon becoming three years of age, gather into vast schools and leave their freshwater nursery grounds, migrating northward along the coast, some as far as the Canadian Maritimes. After a summer of feeding, the bass return to waters near or in their home rivers to wait until the next spring's spawning season. Some of the year's best fishing takes place during these spring and fall migrations.

The Kennebec is a major freshwater drainage in Maine. Five rivers, including the Kennebec itself, converge into a large, tidal, freshwater estuary called Merrymeeting Bay. From Merrymeeting the Kennebec drops 20 miles to the Gulf of Maine. Along its route the Kennebec is nourished by hundreds of tidal creeks and thousands of acres of salt marsh. Outside the Kennebec's 100-foot-deep mouth, sand beaches spread in both directions, where they are entered by smaller rivers with miles of marshland at their heads. This incredible biological factory is truly a paradise for fish. Virtually every important anadromous fish on the East Coast calls the Kennebec home. Like the Hudson, the Kennebec sports both short-nosed and Atlantic sturgeon, as well as shad, spearing, eels, smelts, and all three baitfish-sized herring: alewives, bluebacks, and sea herring (see figure 4.1). It is the huge herring populations—every stage of life is here in abundance—that make the Kennebec extraordinarily attractive to stripers. The Kennebec itself even boasts a spawning population of striped bass. Restored by fingerlings procured in the Hudson, stripers now spawn in the river from which they had been extirpated in the early 1900s, when the Kennebec was befouled by the log drives and the paper companies.

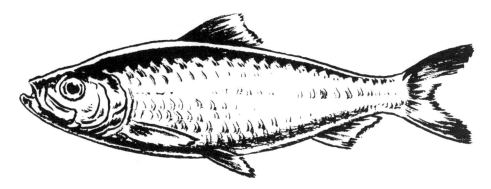

Figure 4.1   Herring are oily, nutritious baitfish.

Many rivers from Maine to the Chesapeake hold stripers. It is the features that we've just discussed, coupled with the Kennebec's incredible fishability, that make it a candidate for the short list of best places. Also, the tremendous freshwater runoff of the Kennebec's tributaries gives the water a tannic coloration. Combine this dark water with the rapid currents that barrel over the river's many ledges and other submerged structures, and you have the perfect daytime feeding environment for striped bass.

The herring schools, drifting with the tides into these feeding stations, create surface-feeding action that has made the river famous. Kib Bramhall, former striped bass fly-rod world record holder from Martha's Vineyard, says that everything else is minor league compared to a Kennebec River striper blitz. Kib and I witnessed three- and four-foot long bass herding herring onto the flats at Fishers Eddy. An army of great blue herons covered the shoreline, and ospreys dived repeatedly into the trapped fish. The surface was covered with the huge boils of the feeding stripers—many of them clearly visible swimming near the boat—and every cast of an oversized, white deceiver brought a jolting strike.

Kennebec fishing depends on the tides. High tide often finds the bass near the marshy shorelines of the river's many bays: Drummore Bay, Winnegance Creek, Heal Eddy, and Back River are just a few of the better ones. Although the entire river system holds stripers, the best availability of larger fish is between Bath and the mouth. Under low-light conditions surface-feeding activity is common on these bays; pay special attention to the outflow areas of the large creeks that are invariably present. These creeks bring baitfish, and the currents provide a feeding station. Often you have only to look for the splashes of feeding stripers or the white shapes of gulls hovering over the action. This surface action is not always confined to the bays; sometimes the hungry stripers can drive bait to the surface anywhere on the river. Even though larger fish can be present—especially if menhaden are around—the predominant sizes of the surfacing fish are less than 30 inches.

Most presentations made to these fish are successful. In the early morning, if conditions are still it may be possible to spook fish by lining them; typically, though, I just toss a cast into the thick of things. When the stripers are hot they'll hit well and are not easily spooked. Poppers will catch fish but often end up back in the fish's gills. A deceiver-type fly, or a Clouser, sized to match the baitfish, will work very well. White, white and green, and yellow are known to be productive colors. Sometimes, when stripers are feeding on smaller baitfish, they become quite picky. Try dead drifting, with no retrieve at all, a realistic fly like an epoxy silverside amidst the feeding fish. The fly may appear to be a baitfish that has been stunned by a predator and is therefore easy pickings. Often, however, the contrarian point of view will work. If you fish a much larger fly than the baitfish that are present, and allow it to sink well below the surface action before retrieving, you may catch the larger fish in the school.

As the tide begins to ebb, the action frequently ceases on the surface. The baitfish and the stripers leave the shallow flats, and the stripers take up residence on the submerged structures to exploit the river's swift currents that bring them food. Green Point, Ram Island, Goat Island, Crow Island Ledge, and Pond Island are among the river's best. Stripers often wait for herring moving downstream with the ebb tide to be squeezed from the 60-foot-deep river channel into the shallow 10- to 25-foot depths of water that lie over the structures.

When working these structures during times of fast current speed, your fly needs to get into the lower half of the water column. Stripers waiting in the slower water near the bottom and behind the structures will not often rise high in the water column for a fly. To get the maximum amount of attractiveness, we use an oversized and overdressed deceiver called the groceries (see figure 4.2). The large fly—sometimes 8 or 10 inches long—shoulders aside a lot of water and appears to be something big enough to be worth the bass's efforts. Cast well up and across the current from your target; ideally your fly should come through the strike zone just off the bottom. This type of fishing will require a 350- to 600-grain sinking-head line. The sink rates vary depending on the weight, but I would count on no more than six inches per second. This means a wait of 20 to 30 seconds for your fly to sink into the strike zone; during that time your fly could drift 60 feet or more downriver. The boat must be positioned so that when the fly has reached strike depth you are in a good position to retrieve. You must consider both wind and current; generally this means casting into the wind so that the boat won't run over your line as it sinks. Plan things so that you retrieve perpendicular to the current's flow; giving your fly the longest possible exposure to fish that are present. Take the time necessary to position yourself for a proper presentation. A single good presentation to the sweet spot cannot be equaled by any number of casts made too far over the fish's head. One additional tip is to

Figure 4.2   *Grocery fly.*

strip right to the surface. Many strikes come just before the end of the retrieve. I can only guess that a striper's instincts are sometimes triggered by a
baitfish that appears to be escaping.

Each of the places that we have mentioned is accessible by a boat, which
you can launch from any of several ramps in or near the small city of Bath. A
solid aluminum boat of 16 feet will do the job, and anything over 20 feet is
too big to be properly maneuverable. To get the most out of the Kennebec a
boat is required; shore accesses are infrequent and not always where you'd
want them. You'll find, however, a couple of worthwhile shore-fishing locations in the lower Kennebec River.

To fish the Kennebec from shore you'll need a navigational chart of the
river as well as a copy of Delorme's *Maine Atlas & Gazetteer,* available nearly
everywhere in Maine. The page of the atlas covering the eastern shore of the
Kennebec below Bath will show the Stein Road. The Stein Road takes you
not only right by Green Point but also to Squirrel Point. Fish both of these
points—and the shoreline near them—during the ebb tide. At Green Point,
fish the upriver side of the point at high tide and then work the rocky finger
of the point itself as the ebb tide gains velocity. At Squirrel Point, both sides
of the peninsula are good producers—the upriver just as it hits the point and
the downriver as it trails off into a flat. Another spot is the beach and the
sandbar running between Fort Popham and Wood Island, on the western
side of the river's mouth. During the dropping tide the whole beach, especially down toward the area where the bar leaves the point, can be good
fishing. Be careful while wading at any of these places since the drop-offs are
abrupt. With a careless step you could be over your waders in swift currents.

For much of the Kennebec's surface action an 8- or 9-weight fly rod is
sufficient and floating or intermediate lines will do the job. For heaving the
groceries and the 350- to 600-grain heads that are necessary to drag these
flies down to feeding depth, you need at least a 10-weight. I prefer an 11 for
lines weighing over 400 grains. I know that you can land 100-pound tarpon
on an 11, but if you hook a 35-pound striper in one of the Kennebec's four-
knot tide rips and are trying to keep him from wrapping you around a rock,
the 11 will seem barely adequate.

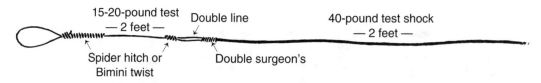

Figure 4.3 *The reverse taper leader works well for large fish that may scrub the leader on bottom structure.*

For surface fishing the standard nine-foot leader with a 15-pound-test tippet will do nicely, and with 20 you can use it for deep presentations. But for deep presentations of the larger flies, I'd suggest a special leader made up in reverse taper (see figure 4.3). Start by tying a Bimini twist in each end of some 20-pound test so that the whole thing is about two feet long, not counting the knots. Leave about a 6-inch loop at the end of each Bimini twist. Now, cut the ends of each loop; double one end over and make a two-strand loop by tying the four strands together with a double surgeon's knot. With a double surgeon's knot, tie the other double-strand end to an 18-inch piece of 40-pound test. This rugged leader allows you to pressure a fish away from the bottom, makes certain that a slow-sinking fly will not be nine feet higher in the water than the sinking head, and gives some needed abrasion resistance should a big bass try to rub your fly out on a rock. Twenty years ago I fished the Kennebec by trolling foot-long swimming plugs on wire line. We used 80-pound-test leaders, and I remember throwing some away after doing battle with just one fish that went over the opposite side of the ledge from the one I was on.

Although stripers are available from May into October, the Kennebec is in its glory in late June. During this time of the year the anadromous herring runs are still winding down, sea herring runs are building, and menhaden are often abundant. The waters are still cool, and the bass are very active. If you can select days in which the high-water slack takes place around daybreak, you've made the best schedule possible.

The weather is usually warm by late June, but this is Maine. Bring along a fleece jacket and warm hat in case it's cooler than normal or damp and foggy.

Although you can certainly fish the Kennebec region without a guide, getting one for a few trips is a great idea. The guides and lodging are centered near the city of Bath. Bath is 40 miles east of the Portland airport on Route 1 or a three-hour drive north from Boston.

Chapter

5

Bonito—
Vineyard Sound,
Massachusetts

*I*n 1944, the Army Air Corps 452nd Bomb Group was based around a concrete air strip built on what had been a cow pasture in Attleborough, England. A bit west of Norwich, Attleborough in those days was a small farm town in the center of the hump on England's far eastern flank, the bulge that pushes out into the North Sea. Our base was located there because it saved our B-17s a few miles when we took off to drop bombs on Germany.

Because Attleborough was so small, there wasn't much for us to do between missions, which is one reason, I suppose, why the 452nd had a fairly decent library. It was there that I found a book that changed my life. Written by Henry Beston, *The Outermost House* is the story of the author's year in a one-room cabin built at the very end of a long, sandy point that pushes into the sea off Cape Cod.

By now, I'm certain, the sea has swept away that driftwood cabin. But the book has endured and become a classic. When I read this lyrical and dramatic tale of life among the elements at the ocean's edge, I was so affected by the author's observant sensitivity to his place in the natural world that I made a promise: if I survived the war, I told myself, I would live the rest of my life on the coast. I would never, I pledged, be far from the sea, its beaches, salt marshes, and rolling dunes that mark the ocean's beginnings.

Except for one year of the 55 since, I've kept that promise. I've lived all those years on the northeast Atlantic coast or in Key West, a small island surrounded by the sea. If you live anywhere in the Northeast you will eventually find your way to Cape Cod and its two largest islands—Nantucket and Martha's Vineyard. And if you are a fisher, you will get there sooner rather than later.

This is how it should be because this is where fishing began. Indeed, it was the first Colonial cod fishermen in their dories and sloops off Cape Cod that saved this young nation from bankruptcy. Those cod, some of them giants by today's standards, became the essential commodity of the colony's trade with England and the rest of Europe. Without that commerce, there would have been no currency in what was to become New England.

In 1712, when Capt. Christopher Hussey's sloop out of Nantucket was blown offshore by a nor'west gale, he found himself alongside a pod of spermaceti whales, one of which he harpooned and brought back to Nantucket Harbor. By the end of the century, the small island had become the whaling capital of the world and enjoyed the prosperity that whaling made possible.

The whales had been hunted down long before the start of the 20th century, but by then the nation had discovered sportfishing. Cape Cod and its islands had a new and different supremacy: they became the saltwater sportfishing capital of the Northeast and one of the most storied sportfishing destinations in the country.

Consider these words written in 1896 by Cape Cod surf caster A. Foster Higgins:

> I had been fishing for some hours without success; and as the now large waves rolled in, my eye followed them, commenting on their remarkable clearness and transparency. I made a new cast and sat down, when on my left, heading for the bait which I had just thrown out, was a beautiful bass, his stripes and silver side plainly visible, his brilliant eyes staring at me, precisely as mine were fixed on him. The wave rolled him up until he was in bold relief against its green depths; and had he been artificially held there, the picture could not have been more perfect or animated. His impetus and intention both carried him as far as the bait. He took it into his mouth, but held it only for an instant and I in vain reeled in and cast again and again.

More than a century later, other Cape Cod anglers are still at it. I know, because although I fished out of eastern Long Island as a young man, I came to the Maine coast more than 40 years ago. And since I've been here, I've been drawn to Cape Cod and its islands by the same magnetism that inevitably pulls every New Englander to these historic places where the eternal sea is such an overwhelming and wondrous presence.

I have walked the breathtaking beaches of Cape Cod National Seashore and watched commercial fishermen mend their nets in Provincetown Harbor. I have been aboard my friend Martin's swordfishing boat out of Woods Hole on the cape, and spent a day there with Frank Mather, one of the world's great fisheries biologists and a lifelong angler with a passion for giant bluefin tuna. My brother Chick's daughter Lindsay was married in the Old Whaling Church on Nantucket, and Chick's oldest son, Charley, wed a Martha's Vineyard lass in Edgartown. Our daughter spent her college summer vacation working in Hyannis. And one of the first plays written by our prize-winning playwright friend Tina Howe opened in Provincetown, long before she was the toast of Broadway.

So you see, I have had many reasons to visit the cape and its two famous islands. And much would have been missing from my life if I hadn't. They are such special places.

But it's fishing, of course, that preoccupied me each time my travels took me to Cape Cod neighborhoods. There is something about the confluence of wind, tides, currents, water temperatures, the course of the Gulf Stream, and the prevailing weather systems in this blessed corner of the Northeast that creates a habitat that shelters more fish per cubic foot of water than any other location northeast of Montauk Point. As for the variety of saltwater fishing venues, no other place the entire length of the northeast Atlantic coast can touch it.

My friend Nelson Bryant, who has written about fishing for more years than most of us have been breathing, lives in West Tisbury on Martha's Vineyard. Even if you have read only a few of Nelson's "Outdoors" columns in the *New York Times,* you know how much this man loves his island home and how much time he has spent exploring and learning its fishing secrets. He doesn't give up these secrets easily, but he shares enough of his discoveries to give all of us some idea of the richness and variety of the angling that's available.

George Reiger, another old-timer like Nelson and me, has written about his friend's first fishing adventure, an experience that set Nelson's course for life.

"Although Nelson Bryant was born in Red Bank, New Jersey, in 1923," Reiger writes in his fine book, *The Striped Bass Chronicles,*

> he caught his first fish on Martha's Vineyard and that made all the difference: he's never wanted to live anywhere else. Shortly before the Battle of the Bulge, where Nelson was wounded for the second time since parachuting into France the night before D-Day, he received a V-mail boost from his dad, who'd just caught a mess of schoolie stripers on trout flies in the Vineyard's Tisbury Great Pond.
>
> After the war, Nelson got work as a deckhand on the research schooner Reliance, based in Woods Hole. In old New Englandish, a hole is neither a hole nor a harbor, but a channel between two islands. In a sense, then, the oceanic arm between Woods Hole and Martha's Vineyard became Nelson's Big Two-Hearted River. He kept a cheap Herter fly rod and Pflueger reel aboard the *Reliance*, which is why the tackle was near at hand when a school of Atlantic

bonito suddenly surfaced one day in Woods Hole harbor. Nelson cast the already attached fly—a Mickey Finn—hooked a seven-pound bonito, and somehow, despite the thicket of pilings around the schooner, landed the fish.

How fitting that one of the region's best-known and best-read fly fishers began his long and productive angling career with a bonito. Because it is a member of the tuna family, a group that swims in every ocean on the planet, the common bonito *(Sarda sarda)* is, pound for pound, one of the strongest fish in the sea. Like its brethren, including the giant bluefin tuna, the albacore, and the yellowfin tuna, the bonito pumps vast amounts of dissolved oxygen into its rich, red bloodstream. It is, like all tuna, an amazingly high-energy, high-metabolism creature, compact as a bullet and nearly all muscle, part of a family that can outswim every creature in all the seas.

At about the same time that Nelson Bryant caught his first bonito on a fly off a boat moored in Woods Hole harbor, I was fishing off Montauk Point with Jimmy Reutershan, my friend and partner. We were aboard his *Peasant,* a 23-foot Jersey skiff, on a sparkling early autumn morning, one of those days when you are charged by the equinoctial energy of the clear air, when it seems as if every living creature must tremble with the sheer joy of being alive.

As we came around the point, trolling handlines for bluefish we hoped to send to Fulton Market, the ocean erupted about a half mile from us just outside the swells that rolled from the open Atlantic. More furious than any feeding frenzy I had ever before seen, what looked like an acre of white water tossed in remarkable tumult. Amid showers of panicked herring hurled skyward in a silver rain, larger fish flashed greenish silver, rocketing here and there with a violent speed quite unlike a school of bluefish or striped bass.

"Look at that, will you!" I shouted. "What could they be?"

"Bonito," Jim answered. "That's a school of bonito."

He pushed forward on the throttle, but by the time we reached the place where the fish had been, there was nothing but scraps of herring here and there in the clear Atlantic and a crowd of gulls and terns screaming as they competed for the tidbits. Then, three-quarters of a mile off, the ocean erupted again.

"There's another school," I shouted.

"Probably the same fish," said Jim. "I'm not going to spend the morning chasing bonito."

He steered his *Peasant* back inside the point and headed for Shagwong where we could see birds circling and diving. "There's our bluefish," said Jim, and he was right.

For the rest of that hard-working day I kept seeing that amazing display on the ocean side of the point, those fish hurtling from the sea, that incredible tumult, that scene of sheer wildness, and I wondered what sort of fish the bonito must be.

Since those long-ago and carefree days, tens of thousands of saltwater fly fishers have discovered the bonito, learned much more about its habits, its feeding cycles, and its migratory patterns. They have also learned that this is still, and probably always will be, one of the strongest and most unpredictable fish of the inshore Atlantic. Several of my fly-fishing friends have said, "If bonito grew as large as striped bass, it would be all but impossible to land them on a fly rod."

When these qualities are combined with the rich historic tapestries and traditions of Cape Cod, Martha's Vineyard, Nantucket, the Elizabeth Islands, Cuttyhunk, Vineyard Sound, and each of the other landmarks and seamarks that have defined for centuries the finest saltwater angling in the Northeast, you have a memorable combination with as much to discover onshore as off. And if the elusive bonito do indeed manage to avoid your flies, don't worry. You'll get another chance.

Tackle and Techniques

It's in part because they are relatively elusive—wild, fleeting creatures of the open sea—that bonito are the most coveted fly-rod fish along the north Atlantic coast. Every year in late July, inshore and even shorebound anglers along Vineyard Sound get a chance to cast a fly into their home waters at a fish that spends most of its life running down prey on the high seas. Sometimes when I see a pod of bonito leaping chaotically as they slip effortlessly through Vineyard Sound's tide rips, I imagine them in winter—out in the Gulf Stream, their silvery sides reflecting like mirrors in the clear, low sunlight. What a thrill it is to catch one here in Vineyard Sound on a fly rod, and to hold such a fish by its rigid, lunate-shaped tail, feeling the muscular firmness of its tunalike body.

Compared with big striped bass, bonito are not large fish; ones over 10 pounds are rare, and few are over 12 pounds. The average bonito available in Vineyard Sound is about 6 pounds. What they give up in size, however, they make up for in the pure horsepower that is common to all the tunalike tribe. Bigelow and Schroeder's *Fishes of the Gulf of Maine* describes the strength of the bonito: ". . . and we can assure the reader that a bonito is one of the strongest fish that swims, weight for weight, and one of the swiftest."

Bonito can grow to nearly three feet in length, and they are about one-fourth as deep as they are long. Like other tunas the bonito has keels on its sides to give support to its powerful tail, and it even has pockets along its body for its fins to retract into for high-speed swimming. The body is firm and muscular. The bonito is easily distinguished from the false albacore—the subject of chapter 8—in that its first dorsal fin is long when compared with the false albacore, and it only gradually tapers back to meet the rear dorsal.

Additionally, the bonito has seven or more dark blue stripes that run forward and down across the lateral line. The common bonito has a very large and prominent eye, as well as a mouth full of sharp, needlelike teeth. When it first comes from the water the bonito is light green, but it darkens to steel blue after death. The sides and underbelly are silvery. The bonito is to my eye one of the most handsome fish in the ocean.

Bonito must spawn nearly as far north as the shores of southern New England because young fish only a few inches in length are seen from time to time in Long Island Sound.

Bonito are also found throughout the warmer parts of the Atlantic Ocean, including the Gulf of Mexico. They are prevalent on both the European and American sides, being common in the Mediterranean and found as far north as Scandinavia. On our coast they are almost never caught north of Cape Cod.

Although many locations along the East Coast offer saltwater fly rodders a shot at bonito, the fishing around Martha's Vineyard is among the best. Bonito can start showing up in the third week of July along the Vineyard's north shore or over on the Cape Cod side. But there's plenty that's not understood about the comings and goings of the bonito. Although the fish arrive as the water temperature approaches the highest of the year, typically above 70 degrees, they become very scarce in September, when the false albacore arrive, but they often return again in October when the water is 15 degrees cooler. There aren't enough false albacore to make it difficult for the bonito to find food; perhaps they simply don't like each other. I have, though rarely, caught both fish from the same school, so I doubt that's the answer. In any case the last three weeks of August have proven themselves to be the most reliable time stretch for bonito, at least in recent years. By early October the false albacore are gone, and the first couple weeks of October are also reasonably reliable producers of bonito.

Bonito probably move inshore during summer because of the warming waters, but they aren't spread evenly throughout southern New England. Places like Vineyard Sound have a uniquely pleasing environment for bonito. First, the currents run at over three knots in much of the sound; this provides an ideal environment for the bonito to use their startling speed simply to run down prey. Second, the sound is home to three of the bonito's favorite prey species: squid, sand eels, and spearing (see figure 5.1). All these baitfish are abundant in the sound during the time that bonito frequent the area. Young of the year fish such as menhaden, herring, and butterfish are also present and may become key forage for bonito.

The shorelines of both Cape Cod and Martha's Vineyard are covered with a succession of shallow, warm, saltwater ponds. Spearing are very abundant in these ponds; these and other baitfish frequently run back and forth between the ponds and the sound. Although I have found a little of everything

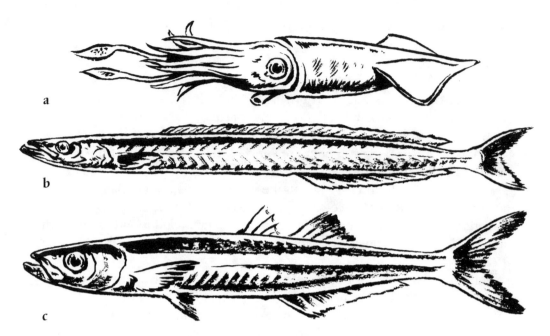

Figure 5.1 (a) Squid, (b) sand eels, and (c) spearing are among Vineyard Sound's top forage.

in the stomachs of the bonito I have taken for the table, it's spearing that are most prevalent. Bonito often disgorge baitfish at the end of a long struggle, allowing a quick prey identification; spearing and sand eels are found more frequently than anything else. An examination of the hottest locations will reveal that many of them are near the entrances to these salt ponds. Waquoit Bay and Eel River on Cape Cod, and Pogue Pond, Edgartown Harbor, Lake Tashmoo, Lagoon Pond, and Menemsha Pond on the Vineyard side are among the most productive of these ponds.

Besides the areas surrounding the ponds, bonito often hold in the sound's many tide rips. The waters between Martha's Vineyard and Cape Cod have a small tidal range but experience rapid current speeds. Essentially, water moves through the sound on its way to filling, or emptying, the larger bodies of water nearby. The bottom of the sound is sandy, and the moving water builds sand hills along the edges of the channels or at various places near shore. As the water flows over these structures the depth can change from 50 feet to 15 feet in only a few yards of surface distance. To pass through these shallows, the water must accelerate dramatically. After the rapidly moving water climbs the sand hill's incline, its velocity causes it to crash into the much deeper and slower moving water just beyond the sandbar's crest. All along the ridge of the shoal a clear line of this turbulence develops. This is called a tide rip. Tide rips are one of the best places to find saltwater game fish, and bonito are no exception. Typically the sweet spot of a tide rip is just a few feet in front of, or right in, that line of turbulence. Powerhouses like jumbo striped bass often come from these rips but seldom rise far from the bottom. Bonito, on the other hand, rocket back and forth through the ocean's fastest water, seemingly without effort. Baitfish, swept into the turbulent shallows, are easy prey for bonito feeding in the rips. Middle Ground, Hedge Fence, and Succonesset Shoals are the names of three often-productive bonito rips.

Pursuing bonito from shore is not impossible, but it's much more difficult than it is from a boat; even a canoe will greatly increase your odds. Occasionally, on the Cape Cod side, bonito are taken from the stone pier in Woods Hole or from near the jetties on South Cape Beach where Waquoit Bay enters Vineyard Sound. These, however, are long shots. On the Vineyard are several places where success is more likely. Either side of Cape Pogue Gut, the beach next to the ferry landing on Chappaquiddick Island where Edgartown Harbor empties out, and both jetties at Menemsha as well as the adjoining section of Lobsterville Beach are the most consistent producers on Martha's Vineyard.

Shoreside anglers will want stripping baskets. This is a fishery where the longest cast you can make is typically none too long; without a basket there's no way to control 80 feet of fly line. You'll also need waders for the beach fishing. Even though you won't be able to wade very far into the water, the waves will surely lap into a normal pair of boots. If you're going to climb around the jetty at Menemsha, you'll want felt soles.

Even a small boat or canoe will be useful. You'll find many days when the bonito will be busting bait in the protected entrances to these ponds that you just can't reach from shore. As calm as all of these places can be on summer days, they can also be nasty and dangerous. Every year some member of the bonito-mosquito fleet gets in trouble off Menemsha; just be cautious. A large aluminum boat or a fiberglass fishing platform suitable for fly rodding will allow you to take in some of the rips as well as the pond entrances. There are often days in which the bonito are simply not showing at one locale, but a tour of the sound's shoreline will reveal a school working in another spot. A boat of 19 or 20 feet equipped with enough power to do 25 knots will help you move around the sound and maximize your chances of finding fish. Fall weather can get out of hand, forcing you to accept a sheltered location, but more often fishers can at least move along the side of the sound on which they launched their boat. The local guides will sometimes make a circle of the sound's shoreline—including two crossings of the sound—to find bonito for their clients.

Although some bonito are caught—usually by fishers using chum—by blind casting to structures, most are taken by casting into fish that are visibly feeding on the surface. Bonito frequently leave the water when chasing bait; their powerful tails create whirlpools, and the fish often somersault in the air, landing randomly with a great splash. The result is that a feeding school of bonito is both incredibly exciting and visible from some distance.

Probably the most debated part of bonito fishing is how to approach these breaking fish. On some days you could run directly into a school of bonito with two huge outboards and never scare a fish. On other days it seems that simply pointing the bow of your boat in the direction of a surfacing school will put them down, as if by telepathy. One thing is for sure, if there's moving water the fish are much easier to approach. I like to run to an upcurrent position from the breaking fish, staying well away from the school. Once I'm in position I'll shut down the motor and let the bonito work toward me. Although the bonito's movements appear erratic, they usually work into the current while feeding. Sometimes you must take the wind into account. In slow-moving water a breeze can push you quietly right into the school. A brisk wind can make casting difficult and boat rides rough, but if I added up all my saltwater days, many of the best were windy. Wind moves boats, baits, and fish; the trick is to use the wind, not fight it.

On some days, however, the fish just don't stay up long enough to allow such a leisurely approach. I've caught more bonito by simply charging up to within casting range of the school, throwing the motor into neutral, and standing up and casting into the action than I have by any other method. Let the motor idle while you make the cast; the time it takes to shut it off could be the difference between success and failure. I've had hundreds of occasions where the breaking fish pushed right by the boat, seemingly oblivious to the running motor.

No matter what your approach it pays to observe the fish. Look for a pattern. A tide rip, eddies in the current of a draining pond, a windy corner of a dock—each can repeatedly host feeding bonito. The bonito will sashay through the bait, scatter it, and disappear, only to return again in 5 or 10 minutes. It may be worth it to anchor within an easy cast of such a spot and wait for your shot. It's also worth knowing that the fish may not really be going anywhere; they may simply be holding in the area, waiting for the bait to gather again.

Whenever bonito have recently left the surface a cast or two into the general area is worthwhile. The fish may still be feeding right there but under the surface. Unless you've got a better place to go I'd wait right there for a few minutes. Frequently the conditions that brought the bonito to the surface initially will cause a feeding spree to reoccur.

The other big giveaway of bonito is the presence of sea gulls and terns, especially terns. Terns feed on sand eels and spearing. When bonito chase this forage to the surface the terns take their share. One of my favorite games is a competition with the terns to be the first to see a reappearing pod of bonito. Frequently, the slightest disturbance by a nervous baitfish—just a ripple or a tiny glint of a scale in the sunshine—heralds a surfacing school of bonito. When I glance quickly at the tern to see if he saw the bait's slight movement, I inevitably find him wheeling about and headed directly for the emerging action. If no birds are canvassing an area it's unlikely that much action is afoot. If, however, birds are patrolling the area, dipping constantly toward the water's surface, then give it a while even if nothing is tearing things up at that moment.

When it comes to casting to bonito keep three things in mind. First, never worry about spooking the fish; they're probably not going to be where you just saw them anyway. Cast right into the thickest part of the action. If they're moving in a direction it will probably be upcurrent. A cast made into a hot school and retrieved into the current is almost a sure thing. Second, you must cast quickly. This is no time for a bunch of false casts. You should approach bonito with the line stripped out, fly in hand, and several feet of head hanging out of the rod tip. Toss the fly and head into the water. With a quick roll cast, and a single backcast, it's possible to throw 60 feet of line. With one more backcast, you can throw 80 or 90 feet. Unlike most fish, when a bonito goes down it may move instantly out of range of your cast, so time is of the essence. Third, learn to cast into the wind forehand and to use the wind to throw your backcast. A common sight during the famous Martha's Vineyard Derby, held in the early fall, is to see expert fly casters false casting into the wind only to shoot extra-long backcasts to fish that have surfaced downwind. Most fly casters don't have a strong enough backcast to load the rod sufficiently if the backcast is into the wind, and if the angle is such that the wind is blowing the backcast onto the angler, he or she may very well catch the hook in the back of the head. Use the wind, don't fight it.

It was once thought that because of the remarkable speed of the bonito all presentations should have a rapid retrieve. But bonito, like all predators, want to expend as little of their precious energy as possible. Many times the most effective technique is simply to cast a realistic-looking fly into the action and allow it to sink slowly, giving it only an occasional twitch back toward the angler. The bonito may mistake this for a baitfish injured during their last foray through the school of baitfish. This kind of slow retrieve will also give you a longer window of opportunity during each cast. Obviously, in fast-moving rips this approach is less practical, especially from an anchored boat. Under these conditions you can dead drift a fly on a sinking line and allow it to swing across the current as a retrieve.

Just this past season I started using a surface slider for casting to breaking bonito. I found that the bonito went wild over the fly as I pulled it along the surface hand over hand at a good clip. The narrow, pointed mouth of the bonito is filled with needlelike teeth, however, and although the bonito's teeth profusely perforated the slider's foam body, the fish were infrequently hooked well enough to land. I'm going to work on this problem, though, because a bonito greyhounding six feet across the water's surface with that slider gripped grimly in its choppers is something I want to see again.

Bonito flies are all fairly small but run the gamut of designs. Because bonito will eat larger baits, something like a three-inch white deceiver should be in your inventory. I've also, unexplainably, seen days when a yellow Clouser about an inch and a half long was particularly effective. In general, though, I have two favorite flies: one is an epoxy pattern, and the other is Bob Popovics's invention called the 3-D (see figure 5.2). I tie the epoxy pattern about an inch and a half long and on a 1/0 hook. The tail is first tied of fly fur, white at the bottom and dark olive green at the top. The sides are formed of reflective tape and then covered with epoxy. I tie my epoxies to be a cross in profile between a sand eel and a spearing. The 3-D is of similar size but is constructed very differently. Small clumps of a crinkly material called super hair are tied at slight angles to the hook shank in alternating layers with a flash material. When finished the semirigid mass is trimmed into the shape of a baitfish. Due to their semirigid shape and reflectiveness, both patterns are effective when dead drifted in a school of breaking fish, my most common presentation to bonito.

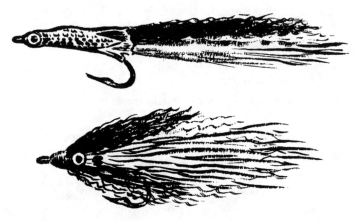

Figure 5.2   *White bait epoxy fly and 3-D silverside fly.*

Bonito, despite their energy, are not big fish, and you generally won't need a rod heavier than a 9-weight. But at anchor, in front of a four-knot tide rip, you might feel differently. If you'll be doing much of that kind of fishing you might want a 10-weight, and you'd be wise to anchor up to a ball that you can quickly release should you hook a fish in all that current. In calm conditions I often use a 6-weight. Later in the season, with more wind or if the possibility exists of hooking larger stripers or blues, I use an 8-weight or 9-weight. An intermediate line will usually take care of things. You can even cast many floating flies successfully on an intermediate. But you should include some 250- or 300-grain sinking-head lines, especially if you'll be fishing in the rips. The most important specification is the backing capacity of your reel. I want *at least* 200 yards of backing on my bonito reels.

The tapered leader that we discussed in chapter 2 will do just fine. I'd suggest a 12-pound-test tippet to start. I frequently use a 15 and can hardly recall losing a bonito due to the leader.

When first hooked a bonito can easily run off a lot of backing, especially if it's a big one. The answer here is not to panic and to have plenty of backing. Don't baby the fish, though; use firm pressure. Bonito have a way of changing direction and suddenly carrying the fight to the opposite side of the boat, along with a couple hundred feet of slack line. Here's where a rapid-retrieve reel can really help. I use a small multiplier that holds 300 yards of Spectra backing; it's a great bonito outfit.

As the bonito approaches the boat it will, like all tunas, swim in tight circles with rapid, throbbing beats of its tail. Take your time. Once the fish is at the boat, skilled anglers often grab it by the tail as it swims tiredly on the surface. It is, however, easy to panic the bonito, resulting in a broken leader. A big freshwater-style landing net is just right for landing bonito at boatside. Beach anglers must slide their fish up on the sand using the same technique we prescribed for stripers. Check the leader carefully after catching a bonito; although the creature's teeth will not cut like those of a bluefish, they can severely abrade a leader. Retie the fly frequently.

The resurgence of striped bass, as well as the popularity of bonito and false albacore, has created a good supply of experienced guides in the Vineyard Sound area. A guide is not vital to the success of a skilled angler, but they can sure help. Bonito are mobile, and today's hot spot may be deserted tomorrow. Sometimes the bonito will establish patterns during which they show at a similar stage of tide for several consecutive days. Because the guides network with each other and are on the water every day, they are likely to know where and when the best fishing will be.

Martha's Vineyard and Cape Cod are both major tourist destinations. August is prime season; September and October are far less crowded. Limited air service is available to both locations. Driving onto Cape Cod, except during the weekend rush, is not a problem; a ferry ride is required to get to Martha's Vineyard. During summer the ferry can be a major obstacle. You can go on standby without advance tickets, which are nearly impossible to get, but you could be in line for hours. Once there, however, you'll see why the place is in such demand.

If you have a decent-sized boat, I'd suggest the cape. There are plenty of accommodations, some with docks, and the towns of Falmouth and Mashpee offer several excellent no-fee ramps. On the Vineyard, you can launch a boat in several of the larger ponds. Both areas have at least a couple of shops that can provide assistance to the visiting saltwater fly fisher.

In August the cape and islands can be very warm, and tropical fishing garb is in order. After Labor Day the weather starts to change, and by mid-October you can experience frost on the deck of a boat in the water. Again the best solution is to wear layers capped with foul-weather clothes, boots, and a warm hat and gloves.

Bluefish— Montauk Point, New York

Bluefish were my first fish. Like other firsts in life, I always remember them, the bluefish and the waters in and around Montauk where I began fishing as a boy and kept at it until fishing helped me, at long last, become a man.

We could, you and I, start at the Shinnecock Canal and head east along either shore of that final finger of Long Island that pokes between the sound and the Atlantic, and we could travel scarcely a mile before we'd discover a bluefish memory.

We could begin on Shelter Island's south shore, there near the ferry slip, there where Dick Hamilton lost most of his gill net, cut down by swift tides, vanished in the dark of a moonless night because bluefish drove him beyond the edge of reason with their frenzied, phosphorescent feeding in those sultry August waters. Or we could leap across to the East End's Atlantic shores where broad sweeps of white sand beach turn truculent as they near Montauk Point, become narrow, rock-strewn strands pounded by ocean swells come to their angry ending in the shadow of Montauk's cliffs. Here I have yanked hooked bluefish from the great curls of those waves, seen countless of their silver brethren suspended there between sea and sky while gulls screamed from all the heavens above.

I could take you aboard Jim's Jersey skiff, his *Peasant*, near Gin Beach just west of Montauk Point along the north shore, there in the bend near Oyster Pond. October's early sunset has begun, but our day is far from ended. Here where the first flashes from Montauk Light gleam through a sudden dusk, we are in the company of bluefish, great schools of them compressed here in this cove by the urgency of their fierce feeding. They have conquered this cove. Their picket line prevents any escape. There is no sanctuary for the schools of sand eels and spearing these blues have herded to their collective doom.

We are, Jim and I, alone amidst the carnage. We are hauling blues over the gunwales on tarred handlines tipped with wire leaders and single-hook cedar jigs, simple lures of sanded, cigar-shaped and cigar-hued cedar plugs with lead heads at one end and a hook at the other. This is market fishing, primitive fishing, not far removed from the way of the early colonists, who caught the ancestors of these very fish on hand-whittled wooden lures.

What you cannot see, perhaps, in your mind's eye are the aspects of fever that grip us both. You must experience bluefish for that, for there is something in the sheer unbridled wildness of their presence that pumps great slugs of adrenaline through our systems. It is a kind of madness, a portrait of universal excess. Above us in the dusk terns scream, their raspy shrieks charged with a wild hysteria as they plunge into the bluefish maelstrom, gorging on lacerated spearing. Mixed with the terns are herring gulls, laughing gulls, great black backs, and more—one vast, disorderly flock milling like so much chaff tossed in a cyclonic storm.

Six tarred lines trail beyond the *Peasant's* no-nonsense stern—three for each of us, Jim starboard, me on the port. Each of the outermost lines stretches from a stubby outrigger, and each has a slice of innertube knotted into its length just above the waterline. When a bluefish strikes and hooks itself, the resilient rubber stretches, giving just enough slack so the hook will not be ripped from bluefish jaws by the boat's forward motion.

There is no science to this. We are in it for the meat. These bluefish are our livelihood. Besides, there is no time for reflection. Trolling at the edges of the shifting schools, we must deal with almost constant hook-ups. One of the three lines is always in our hands as we haul hand over hand, our strength and energy against the wild strength and ultimate energy of the 8- to 12-pound bluefish that we yank clear of the transom and flip into one of the open fish boxes on the 23-footer's aft deck.

Slippery with the partially digested remains of baitfish disgorged by boated blues, wet with the slime and seawater mix that sloshes in the scuppers, the slick deck tests our balance and our concentration. Our gloved hands are cramped by the constant damp of chill water; our flannel shirts and yellow oilskin pants gleam with the scales of nearly 400 pounds of bluefish we have horsed across the transom.

Ours is a manic routine, fueled by adrenaline and the knowledge that if we are to make even a token wage for our labor, we must hook and boat as many bluefish as possible during the short time the fish will crowd this cove. A shift in the wind, a change in the tide, or any number of unseen natural events beneath the roiled surface can, in a manner of minutes, end the frenzy that surrounds us. Where there was white water thrashed by surface feeding there will, in the blink of an eye, be nothing but a spreading silver slick, sweet smelling with oils of shredded silversides. Some say the odor reminds them of ripe watermelon just split open. Others, and I am one, say the heavy smell, rotund in its richness, is unique to bluefish.

And with good reason, for I have seen the sheen of a small slick blossom from below, spreading slowly across calm waters as if an unseen hand poured oil from above. It is the smell—that peculiar, unique bluefish smell—that tells me there is slaughter underway far beneath. Some anglers have laughed when I claim I smell bluefish, but they are not disbelievers for long.

There in that October dusk, the sweetness lay heavy on the air until it became part of us, part of our soaked clothing. We and the bluefish were becoming one: we wore their scales, we were stained with their blood and slime, we smelled of their smell.

When the fish had left, we had those reminders of their reality. Where minutes before there had been carnage, now there was only silence. Where countless birds had screamed, only a desolate, silent few swooped here and there for the final scraps. Bluefish are like that, especially in Montauk's turbulent tides. As suddenly as a lightning strike, they slash to the surface, herding shoals of bait with whips of panic. Then they are gone, vanished like smoke in a gale.

We head for the lights of the breakwater at the entrance to Montauk Lake. We have hours of work ahead of us: gutting, washing, weighing, boxing, and icing every bluefish, closing and labeling the boxes for shipment to Fulton Market. Then, in the long day's final chore, we scrub down and wash the *Peasant* until she and her decks are shed of every scale, cleansed of every trace of gurry. She is ready for her tomorrow off the point, a tomorrow now just hours from becoming.

How many days and nights like that did I spend with Jim and bluefish more than 50 years ago? They are beyond counting. They have become just one of the many bluefish dramas that play out over all these years on the vivid stage of my fishing memories. And they are made more unforgettable because a bluefish was my first fish, and you never forget your first.

I was 10, perhaps 11, when a friend invited my brother Chick and me to join her and her two sons on a snapper fishing excursion to the Three Mile Harbor breakwater. We had long, bamboo poles tipped with a 10- or 12-foot length of line, then a gut leader and a long-shanked, snelled hook. A bobber three feet above the hook would be tugged below when a snapper blue struck the spearing on the hook. That's what I was told just before I was handed a pole.

I flipped the baited hook and bobber into the swift tide there near the breakwater's end, all the water of Three Mile racing through the narrow channel to empty into Gardiners Bay. I could not visualize how any fish could conquer such a current. Yet as my bobber drifted swiftly, it was yanked beneath the swirling surface and there was life surging, struggling at the end of my line. As the bamboo bowed, I pulled and at last there came a flashing being from the sea, swung crudely ashore to the breakwater's boulders where I fell on it, clutched it with both hands and would not let go until a bucket was brought to hold that three-quarter-pound snapper blue, the feisty offspring of those adults I would meet off Montauk a quarter century later.

By then, I was the parent, not the child. Yet I brought our son, Marshall, to Three Mile when he was barely three. He could hold a bamboo pole, and he managed to swing his first snapper ashore. He thought enough of that first fish to keep it beside him in his crib all through that night.

When I see bluefish, I see my life.

Sixty-five years after that day at the breakwater I return to Montauk, a guest now, a fly fisher, not a meat fisher. Some things have changed, but many have not. Yes, there are more homes planted on the Montauk hills, homes that nudge at the edges of the cliffs, homes that risk disaster but gain the sweeping vistas of the open ocean in return. There are many more risk takers; that much has changed.

But the graceful, spoon-shaped length of Montauk Lake still lies cupped in the palm of the point's gentle hills, and the breakwaters there at the west end of Gin Beach still frame the lake's entrance, one of the busiest fishing-boat passages in the Northeast. The Montauk Point Light still stands above the turbulent confluence of this place of churning waters where the sound and the Atlantic collide at the migratory crossroads of vast schools of bluefish, striped bass, albacore, weakfish, bonito, fluke, sea bass, menhaden, anchovies, spearing, sand eels, and more. This has not changed, and Montauk Light still presides even though the sea has eroded much of the bluff it was built on. One of these decades, the sea will claim this light.

But on this fine June morning no one is worrying much about that. We are thinking fishing, and the years tumble into the wake of Paul Dixon's flats skiff as he puts her up on a plane just as we clear the Montauk Lake breakwater. He gives the reef at Shagwong a glance, checks to see if any birds are working off Culloden, then makes a decision and heads west to Napeague. The tide is right for poling the flats in Napeague Harbor, where blues may be feeding on the ebb tide at the mouth of the channel.

For me, the skiff is racing back through time. On one side are the cliffs of Hither Hills, on the other, the hills of Gardiners Island and the pale, slim sand spit that is Cartwright Shoals. These waters are my history. I have spent days and nights and days again aboard other boats chasing bluefish and the bright white snow showers of terns that whirl screaming above their thrashing multitudes. There is not a single hour of any of the 24 that I have not patrolled these waters. From darkest nights when heat lightning tore holes in the black sky to sultry dawns when a red sun reluctantly lifted free of the eastern horizon and then set 15 hours later behind the black line of the Northwest Woods—I have been here through it all and more. This has got to be one of the fishiest places on the planet. That much I have learned.

So I am pleased, but not surprised, when I first see the white knot of terns whirling tight against the June-blue sky, out there to the northwest off Cartwright's western tip, where tides churn at sudden, sandy shoals.

Bluefish are at the center of this white-water tempest. We see the flash of pale silver flanks surfacing in the sun as the blues churn amongst hapless schools of panicked sand eels. This is fly casting made easy. One back cast, perhaps two: I need only clear the line on the deck, get the Clouser in the water, let it drift downtide. Then one strip, then two perhaps, and white water geysers as a bluefish strikes.

So wanton is their frenzy that more often than not they will miss that first slashing attack. Not to worry. If that fish turns away, another takes its place. There is this wondrous constancy to the turmoil. It's as if some impossibly high musical note is sounding, higher than you thought you'd ever hear, and it just keeps coming, an excitement sustained beyond your imagining. Feeding blues can do this. For there is something so elemental, so purely savage in their chopping that even an angler of my considerable years and innumerable bluefish encounters is still caught up in the moment as the terns scream and bluefish thrash at the fly.

All other fish are exciting, yes. They are to me, anyway. But a school of feeding blues carries me beyond the norm. They always have, these bright wild beings.

There is no depth here at Cartwright, six feet, perhaps, at the most. A hooked blue has no place to run but out, and off they go, taking me into the backing faster than I thought possible. These are not large fish, four to five pounds, yet they surge with the sudden and surprising force that is the bluefish hallmark. A pure vitality communicates the length of the taut line. You are in touch with life, no doubt about it.

We are fishing single, barbless hooks. Given slack, once alongside the skiff, most of the fish slide free. One does not. I reach to lift it, and the feel of its pulsing quiver in my hand is a signal from the past, a reprise of those countless blues of Montauk that have come over the gunwales of a score of boats. But this one is different. A gentle tug with my pliers and the hook is out. I drop this blue back into the sea and it vanishes, gone free as the sundance on the surface.

There is, I know, no penance for all the dead bluefish of my past. But I tell myself it is good to give these blues their liberty. I have known them and this place for 65 years now, ever since that autumn afternoon at Three Mile. I am a lucky man to be finding them still, especially here at Cartwright where so many other small dramas of my fishing beginnings played out.

Thirty minutes later, the terns lift, the gulls fly off, and the fish are gone. This is how it is with blues. At some silent signal no one else can hear, they abandon their attacks. They go, that's all. Yes, they were here. But now they're gone. Face it, that's what bluefish do.

Big water, I have learned, often holds big bluefish: monsters, Godzilla blues, 15- to 20-pound tackle busters. Twenty miles due north of Montauk Point is Race Rock, just off the west end of Fishers Island. This is another spot where the waters of Long Island Sound meet an edge of the Atlantic. As at Montauk, the constant tides run deep, and as at Montauk, there are almost always Godzilla blues in the depths. They are, however, difficult for any angler, with any equipment, to catch. For a fly rodder, they are all but out of reach.

Nevertheless, they are there. Sometimes they'll surface, most often in early autumn when cooling water temperatures prompt them to store up some excess fat to energize their approaching migration. This is when you want to be "under the light," as they say on the East End, preferably in a sound, seaworthy boat that can hold her own just in back of the Atlantic's rolling surf, those combers that crash so constantly against Montauk's rocky beaches.

If you've been living right and are lucky, those monsters will show for you. But be careful what you wish for. I cast a fly into Montauk's white water one early October morning and wham! I was connected. It was one of those gorillas. I never learned how large. That big bluefish spooled me and was gone.

I'm grateful there are so many others in the creel of my Montauk memories.

Tackle and Techniques

Bluefish have been given the nickname saltwater piranha, and if ever there were a fish with an attitude, this would be the one. Armed with the densest and sharpest set of choppers—another nickname—in the business, nothing short of steel can stand up to attack by bluefish. I've seen bluefish herding menhaden up Maine's tidal rivers, the atmosphere being sheer bedlam. The small shiny menhaden, frantic for any quarter, leapt, sometimes onto dry land, from the surface of a river running red with their blood. Under these conditions bluefish will hit any lure that is presented. After a contest that combines brute strength and amazing agility—for bluefish can jump and tail walk—a modest percentage of the fish initially hooked are brought into the boat, thrashing wildly. Even out of the water they continue to roll their big yellow eyes while their jaws snap automatically at anything in reach. I've walked by a boated bluefish, and watched its eyes following me. When a stick is held near enough, I've seen them lift the front half of their bodies off the deck and take a vicious snap at it. The bluefish is one tough customer.

The bluefish is also a superior fly-rod game fish. For one thing, bluefish grow to over 20 pounds, and three and one-half feet in length. I've caught many high-teen-sized blues on flies, and their fight is terrific. Bluefish, no matter what the size, don't seem to run in the same direction for long; their darkly colored muscles, however, give them great endurance. Bluefish will lie on their side, much like a tuna, and become unbelievably difficult to bring close to the boat.

The bluefish is also a versatile predator; they can be taken from the top of the water column to the bottom, and they're readily available to shoreside anglers. Perhaps the most thrilling spectacle in bluefishing is to see one of these big devils crashing a large popper. The power and determination behind their strike is thrilling; the weekly fishing magazines refer to the excitement that bluefish create in anglers as "bluefish fever."

Of all our top 10 selections in this book the bluefish's habits are the least predictable. One old writing referred to their seasonal appearances, or lack of, as "capricious movements." Blues are infinitely more dependable south of Cape Cod than in the Gulf of Maine. Even on New York's Long Island, blues have been nonexistent for periods long enough that middle-aged folk could not identify one caught at the town dock. This has certainly not been the case in the last half of this century. As we move toward the new millennium, bluefishing is hot at Montauk.

Capricious movements aside, blues generally make an appearance at Montauk in the middle of May, and schools of blues are normally abundant until late October or early November. Bluefish, though, are really a warm-water fish; some are taken as far south as Cuba and over into the Gulf of Mexico. At least some of the fish that frequent the Northeast may go offshore as much as they do south. Deep-water trawls have taken blues in the middle of winter as close as the edge of the continental shelf directly offshore from New York. But bluefish tagged in New York have also been recaptured in Cuba. Perhaps it's fitting that the bluefish belongs to no family of fish. Its closest relatives may be members of the jack family, also southern fish. But when they made bluefish, they threw away the mold.

Bluefish spawn near Montauk; that's clear due to the presence of snapper, or young-of-the-year, blues in virtually every salt pond and estuary in Long Island Sound. Snapper blues themselves support an important sport fishery. I can think of no other game fish that makes as desirable a target in its first year of life. Snapper fishing starts in August as the fish reach six or eight inches in size, and it continues into the fall until the young blues venture out onto the coast. Fishing for snappers with a half of a mummichog and a bobber has introduced thousands of children to the joys of saltwater fishing. I've had some fun with snappers by casting a tiny white streamer on a three-weight fly rod. And snappers are delicious table fare.

Montauk is the perfect place for blues of all sizes and for fly fishers of all persuasions. Off the point, the tumbling tide rips hold the largest fish. The rocky beaches near the light provide the perfect shoreline for the blues to hem in schools of migrating baitfish. Just west of the point the relative placidness of the sound can lend an almost estuarine aura to the fishing. On each tide, water moves by Montauk, on its way to either filling or emptying Long Island Sound; virtually every kind of baitfish found in either the mid-Atlantic or the Northeast migrates through these waters at some time during the season. Montauk is a well-stocked larder for the voracious and versatile bluefish.

Blues do have their favorite forages though. Even in recent years, when few menhaden venture to New England, Montauk has held some schools. This big, oily baitfish is certainly number one in the bluefish's book. Montauk also has herring, although later in the season, and mullet; both are good sized, oily, nutritious baits preferred by bluefish. Butterfish and squid are numerous at different times during the season. Additionally, Montauk not only hosts the sand eels and spearing that are abundant farther north but also has a solid fall run of bay anchovies (see figure 6.1). The bay anchovies become so thick that they create the appearance of an amorphous, brown stain on the water's surface. On the right days in October, Montauk's waters are literally alive with massive schools of blues, ripping their way through the tightly packed schools of anchovies. Flocks of gulls that number in the thousands hang over the surface of the water; the commotion can be seen for miles as you approach the point.

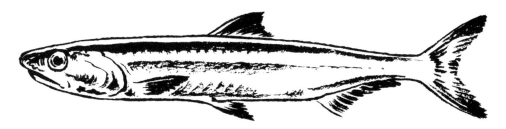

Figure 6.1 *Bay anchovies create Montauk's fall surface blitzes of bass and blues.*

Montauk Point offers shore fishers an excellent chance to hook large fish— both blues and striped bass. It is perhaps the best opportunity on the Northeast Coast. A four-wheel-drive vehicle can be helpful, but it is not necessary, especially near the light or along the south side where there is no beach driving. Much of the Montauk area is held in state parks; this is an advantage for shore access.

We'll start our summary of Montauk's shore-fishing opportunities at Shagwong Point. Shagwong Point extends well into Long Island Sound to become a large underwater reef. It's not unusual for schools of blues to come right ashore at Shagwong, sometimes enveloping wading anglers in blues and baitfish.

Running east we next come to the connecting structures of North and False bars. Here, on the outgoing tide a considerable rip develops that can bring plenty of feeding fish within range of fly fishers. This is a big structure that can hold many anglers.

The area right under the light itself provides no place to backcast, but on either side of the light are Scott's Hole to the west and Turtle Cove around the point to the south. Both can be the scenes of some tremendous inshore action, as can the long section of boulder-strewn beach continuing down the south side away from the light. Adventuresome anglers wade out, then crawl up onto boulders, providing themselves with near-private access to some of the best water that a fly rodder could hope to reach from the shore. Access to the south side is through Montauk State Park, near the lighthouse, and Fort Hero, which has space for campers.

As good as the beach fishing is at Montauk, fishing from a boat is even better. In many cases you can still access fish that are near the beach, but you can also chase schools feeding on the surface farther offshore, or even drift while blind casting with a sinking line in the rips. Montauk is a popular spot, especially on weekends. Boat fishers who get too close to the shore will find themselves the targets of missiles from the beach, as well as a profane, verbal fusillade. If you fish from a boat you'll have plenty of other options that are a safer distance from the surf casters.

Blues at Montauk can be almost anywhere. If you don't see birds working over fish, then you must settle down to working the structures. I've had some very productive fishing by simply drifting all along the massive area of 15- to 25-foot deep water that runs east from Shagwong and then wraps around the point. Most experts like an ebb tide, with the current exiting the sound, for this fishing. Casting a 400-grain head and a grocery fly, as you drift with the current over the boulder-strewn bottom, you'll often make contact with big bluefish and stripers. Give this setup the 15- or 20-second sink time that it needs to get into the strike zone. I find that a long strip creates the impression of movement in the fly that incites the predator to strike. Keep an eye on your depth recorder; schools of fish should be clearly visible at these modest depths. If you run over a good school that produces a strike, it's worth it to interrupt your drift to run back up for another try over the structure. When I get a strike in this kind of fishing I not only note the bottom formations shown on the recorder but also try to mark my position with landmarks. Buoys and shoreside structures are numerous enough to permit a reasonably accurate fix. Don't forget to allow for the effects of wind and tides.

Another area to try from a boat if surface action isn't visible, or if you don't care for sinking-line fishing, is the boulder field that lies just off the beach and runs around the point and down the south shore. Prospecting as close to the rocks as you can get with a large deceiver and an intermediate line can produce excellent action, especially on a flood tide. Look for fingers of current running near the rocks or birds resting on seaward boulders. These spots have a higher-than-average likelihood of holding bluefish.

If the fish are clearly visible feeding on the surface, your job is easier. The moving waters of the point and the large schools of game fish there usually mean aggressive fish. That doesn't mean that bluefish are never selective; at times they can be frustrating. This happens typically in calm waters and when the fish are on small baitfish. When the baitfish are small, I've had my best luck by throwing a fly much larger than the bait into the feeding fish, letting it sink a few feet, and stripping like crazy. You'll certainly know quickly if this approach will work. Sometimes, you'll see the blues lazily rolling through the thickly packed smaller baitfish, and the big-fly thing won't work. In this case you'll have to match the hatch. Flies like the ones that I suggested for bonito, perhaps colored brown, and tied only one and one-half inches long as anchovy patterns will often do it. If the strikes are slow in coming but you do take a fish, see if it regurgitates some of the baitfish that it's been eating. Sometimes I'll put a captured blue in the livewell for a few minutes; this will usually provide a sample of the bait. Use whatever you have to cut your fly to shape and size. Normally the profile and the retrieve, more than the exact appearance of the fly, are responsible for success. When blues are stuck on tiny surface baits it's hard to beat a floating line, a presentation made well away from the boat, and a dead-drifted or very slowly retrieved fly to get action. If all else fails, blues are often a sucker for a big, noisy popper yanked loudly along the water's surface. The fish can't see poppers well, but they know they're big, and they must think that they're large baitfish desperately trying to get away. Have some of these poppers in colors like blaze orange; we're talking attractors here. God only knows what the bluefish think they are, but they work. Casting into a school of frenzied bluefish requires one other unique bit of advice. Unless it's glass calm I doubt that you'll spook bluefish by casting into them. You should, however, not cast deep into a school of feeding blues because other blues may inadvertently bite your line in half as they thrash open mouthed into the bait. I've seen it happen on several occasions.

I tie no flies specifically for bluefish; the flies that we've already suggested for striped bass and bonito can effectively cover the baitfish that you'll find at Montauk. You should know, however, that a bucktail and feather combination like the deceiver will be quickly ruined by the teeth of a bluefish. To some fly tiers this is a joy in itself, providing a reason to tie more flies. If this isn't you, however, you may want to use flies tied with artificial fibers and epoxy bodies; they'll take a lot of chewing. Bob Popovics has told me that he developed epoxy flies with tough synthetic materials so that a good number of bluefish could be caught on the same fly (see figure 6.2). Hook sizes range from size 1 for the bay anchovy patterns up to 4/0 for grocery flies for blind casting to deep structures. A long-shanked hook can be used for bluefish flies; just tie farther back on the hook to gain an extra measure of protection against being bitten off.

Figure 6.2   *Epoxy bay anchovy fly.*

Like the fish themselves bluefish tackle can run the gamut of sizes. If you know that you are going to be working on bluefish of under five or six pounds, and in calm waters, then a rod as light as a 6- or 7-weight is fine. If, however, you're prospecting around, and a mix of sizes is present, you'll want at least an 8-weight, and probably a 9 or 10. I'd suggest a 10-weight for shore fishing, especially near the rocks; it'll seem like a toothpick if a 15-pound bluefish grabs your fly.

If you're concentrating on bluefish, a wire trace at the end of your leader is a good idea. The trace need not be more than six inches long. You can keep a fly wallet with some flies made up that have these wire tips fastened on with a haywire twist (see figure 6.3). Alternatively, you can tie a length of wire to your fly and fix a small snap, as used by spin fishers, on the end so that you can change flies. To some this may sound almost sacrilegious, but I know one of the top names in our sport who has done this for years, even attaching a snap to the monofilament ends of his striper leaders. You can also use 40-, 50-, or even 80-pound-test bite tippets. They will, however, interfere with the fly as much as or more than single-strand 20- or 30-pound-test stainless wire, and bluefish can bite right through rope-sized mono. Tuna fishers curse bluefish. A school of Godzilla blues will often rise up and bite through 100-pound-test, or greater, mono, denuding a squid spreader rig of $15 rubber squids in a few seconds. This is ironic because giant tuna love to feed on adult bluefish.

Remember two important things about fighting and landing bluefish. First, bluefish have incredible stamina, and you must have patience to land a large one on a fly rod. I've seen many fly rods broken on bluefish as anglers

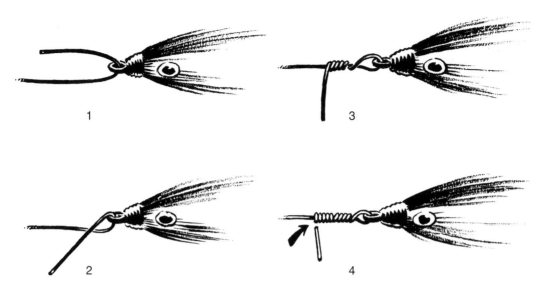

Figure 6.3   *The haywire twist. The original recipe calls for twisting the tag end of the wire back and forth until it breaks at the twist—easier said than done. The author cuts off the tag end with wire clippers.*

became anxious about landing their prize and lifted their rod tip too far backward. Take your time and keep your rod angle low—this will put the pressure on the butt, where it belongs. Besides, you don't want to deal with a bluefish that's still feeling his sand eels. Second, you must avoid the teeth of a bluefish. The safest way to handle bluefish is to gaff them, but this isn't the best way if you plan to release them. And blues will absolutely destroy a landing net. The best way to handle them is to grab them carefully, but firmly, behind the head and use a long pair of stout pliers to unhook them without bringing them into the boat. Many people have been deeply cut by bluefish that have slid and flopped their way along the bottom of the boat until arriving undetected at the toes of an angler stricken with bluefish fever.

Montauk is big water. When the tide running out of Long Island Sound and across the shoals off the light meets the onshore swells of the North Atlantic, an awesome and dangerous rip can form. In even moderate winds, the waters near the point require a mid-20-foot boat and a knowledgeable captain. The waters back from the rip and toward Shagwong are not to be underestimated but are less likely to be life threatening. Like most of these areas, you can fish them effectively on your own, but a guide—at least for a trip or two—is a good idea.

Montauk, unfortunately, is within a couple of hours of driving time from New York City. When the fishing is good, it can be crowded from either shore or boat. You will definitely see some "me first" kind of people headed for the fastest action, regardless of who or what is in the way. If you can bring yourself to move away from that exact spot, though, the place is big enough and good enough that you'll be able to enjoy yourself. The flip side of the nearby urbanization is the infrastructure for handling all those people. The area contains numerous motels, and because much of the eastern end of Long Island is held in parkland the access is quite good. Above all, Montauk may be the best fishing spot in the Northeast and one of the top two on the East Coast.

The clothing advisory for Montauk is the same as that for Vineyard Sound. The two places are only about 40 miles apart by water.

Chapter
7

Weakfish— Barnegat Bay, New Jersey

The canoe and kayak launch site near the southern end of New Jersey's Island Beach State Park is on the north shore, the north side, of the nine-mile long barrier beach that separates Barnegat Bay from the open Atlantic. If you want to wade and cast flies for weakfish—or striped bass, for that matter—this is a convenient starting point. Anglers who drive the length of the park's only paved road can find convenient parking just a short walk from the launch site, and the bay's shallows here are good weakfish water: shoal and grassy.

On an early September day as the sun blazed bright in a cloudless, midday sky, I opted for relaxing in the lee, out of the brisk southwest breeze. Shielded from the wind's husky presence, I could enjoy the sun's surging warmth even as I knew this could well be one of the last days of the year when an elderly body like mine could luxuriate in the blessings of a waning summer. A cold front had moved through the previous day, riding hard on a charging northwest wind, blustery and rudely chilled. This was not a good wind for weakfish, which, like me, cotton to gentle airs and balmy days and nights.

As I watched a flight of three black ducks circle low and fast as they approached a landing in a nearby freshwater pothole, a young man appeared carrying waders, a fly rod, and a knapsack that held his reels and accessories. I said hi, as did he, and I watched as he pushed into his waders, threaded a leader through his rod guides and carried out the rituals of making ready.

"Where are you from?" I asked, as he began his fly-selection deliberations.

"I'm from here in New Jersey. Actually, I grew up not far from here. But," he said, looking up from his flies, "I moved to Hoboken not long ago. I work in the city, and the move cuts almost a half hour from my commute."

Once our exchange had come this far, we began a full-fledged conversation. Turns out he was a stockbroker on a week's vacation from Wall Street's constant tensions. His discovery of fly fishing's therapeutic benefits had been recent. A graduate of a regional fly-fishing class, he had certainly learned what equipment and accessories were considered proper. He looked ready to pose for an advertisement in an Orvis catalog, right down to the flies tucked into the sheepskin flap on his fly-fisher's vest. And he was full of enthusiasm, quite undismayed by the stiff breeze, the dazzling sun, or reports that the previous day's nor'west gale might have driven the bay's weakfish to deeper waters.

When I ventured an opinion on the probable weakfish drought, the young angler replied, "Hey, it doesn't really matter to me. Sure, it would be great to hook up, but what I really wanted was a chance to get away, to be out here on the water, casting.

"And look," he said, sweeping one hand the length of the bay shore, "there's no one else around. I'm the only guy fishing here. That means everything to me, especially when the city is just a few miles up the coast. Imagine having a beach all to yourself this close to New York."

Selecting and attaching a yellow and white Clouser to his light leader, he said his good-byes and waded off onto Barnegat Bay's extensive shoals.

I wonder, I asked myself as he left, if he's aware of the coincidence of his fishing adventure and the history of Island Beach State Park. For had it not been for the misadventures of another financier, this young man might never have found such wild solitude so close to one of the world's largest cities.

Like so many Americans in 1926, especially in the Northeast, Henry C. Phipps, a steel magnate from Pittsburgh, thought the good times would last forever. America had just helped win a world war, the stock market belonged to the bulls, and an entire generation of New Yorkers dreamed of owning vacation homes, places they could reach in less than a day's travel, thanks to faster trains and the wonders of the recently arrived motorcar, especially the people's automobiles being built by Henry Ford in Detroit.

Anyone with lots of money to invest looking at Island Beach in those days could see its potential. Barnegat Bay was already known as a premiere duck-shooting and fishing spot. Some of the most luxurious gun clubs in the world were built on the bay's shores and its southernmost islands. Less than 50 miles south of Wall Street as the crow flies, the bay's abundant natural resources, its teeming waterfowl and wildlife, its blueclaw crabs and its fisheries, were known to an entire generation of America's first sports participants: men and women who hunted and fished, not for sustenance but for the sheer enjoyment of the experience.

In the vision of Henry Phipps, these were the people who would be eager to buy land and build stylish homes on his narrow, lovely strip of white sand and rolling dunes, anchored by patches of pitch pine, holly, and bayberry. Embroidered with tidal marshes, highlighted here and there by postage-stamp freshwater ponds, and washed its entire length by both the bay and the ocean, Island Beach must have been a speculator's dream. Anyone who can imagine the frenzy of the go-go '20s can also recreate the moment Henry first sat down with his charts of the island and began sketching in property lines, dollar signs, and dreams of glory.

Alas, it was not to be. Like so many captains of industry and adventurers in stock-market speculation, Mr. Phipps was smitten with acute cash-flow problems shortly after the crash of 1929 and the start of the Great Depression. Following Henry's death in 1931, taxes on Island Beach were no longer insignificant, and in 1933 then Governor Harry Moore signed an act that created the Borough of Island Beach, a necessary preliminary to development. But in 1953, in what was one of New Jersey's most foresighted decisions, the state bought the land from the Phipps heirs and officially opened it to the public as a state park in 1959. Unlike many parks, this one was designed to be kept wild and undeveloped.

Happily for all who love the open ocean beach much as it has been since the beginning of time, Island Beach has been handled with care, foresight, and meticulous attention to maintaining its environmental integrity. It is the only wild beach in New Jersey and one of the few anywhere along the Northeast Coast.

This is one good reason why it is a favorite angler's destination. And there are more. For even though most of the Jersey shore now supports side-by-side beachfront homes, restaurants, ice-cream stands, delicatessens, service stations, liquor stores, and motels as far as the eye can see, the particular stretch of the Atlantic Ocean that breaks on this shore has always been, and still is, home to some of the finest saltwater fishing on the continent. The proximity of the Gulf Stream and cold Atlantic currents combine to generate waters rich in plankton, which, in turn, supports vast schools of small crustaceans and, one step up in the food chain, hordes of baitfish like sea anchovies, small menhaden (known as peanut bunker along the beach), sand eels, silversides, and more.

The rest is history, literally. Drawn by the inshore proximity of great schools of striped bass, bluefish, weakfish, fluke, bonito, and albacore, pioneering saltwater fly casters trekked to the Jersey shore, especially the communities around Barnegat Bay. Legendary anglers like Lefty Kreh, Van Campen Heilner, Lee Wulff, and their peers gathered in New Jersey shore communities like

Seaside Park, Ocean Beach, and Point Pleasant. That heritage of almost a half century ago prevails today. Bob Popovics, one of saltwater fishing's finest fly tiers does his work in the modest second-floor studio of his Seaside Park home, a place that has become a Mecca for hundreds of anglers the length of the coast. They knock and walk in. They know they're welcome because Bob is that kind of guy.

Tom Fote's home is almost within walking distance, easily identified by the four-wheeler parked in the driveway. Like so many Jersey coast vehicles, it's festooned with rod holders and sports a tackle box the size of a steamer trunk on the front bumper. Tom came to fish. He's also the tireless CEO of the Jersey Coast Anglers Association, the outfit that has worked so effectively to protect and ensure the long-term viability of the natural resources that enrich this remarkable stretch of coast. Take a ride with Tom as he scouts the surf line and you'll learn more about fishing this beach in 30 minutes than you could during 30 days on your own.

If you can't work in the Fote Grand Tour, don't worry. You'll always be welcome at Betty and Nick's Bait and Tackle on Central Avenue in Seaside Park. The moment you open the door, you'll know you've come to a place that's focused on fishing and the anglers who pursue it. For more than 25 years, the place has been an unofficial angling headquarters and more. Besides gear of all kinds and up-to-the-minute fishing information and consultation, Betty and Nick's serves breakfast before the sun rises and keeps serving hearty food and hot coffee until after it sets. And where else can you get fishing reports that are updated every day, along with the latest Nexrad satellite weather photos. As owner John Bushell Sr., says, "We provide our customers with the best service and personal attention. We're dedicated to offering personalized service to every angler."

But not even the combined skills of Tom Fote and the folks at Betty and Nick's could have helped me bring home a weakfish from the waters off Island Beach. I was too content to sit in the warm sun, out of the wind, where I could recall the weakfish of my youth.

"When the lilacs bloom in May
The weakfish are in Peconic Bay."

That bit of doggerel echoed through my early teenage years. During those years, anglers from North Carolina to eastern Long Island could count on weakfish migrations that guaranteed good fishing all along the coast. But my brother Chick and I were away at school until the wonderful spring of 1941 when, as graduating seniors, we could escape just in time for some late May weakfishing.

In those days, a great deal changed when a teenager reached 18. In New York state we became eligible for our first driver's licenses—a remarkable transition. The world suddenly seemed under our control, not our parents'. It was quite a difference from our recent past.

What a joy it was to exploit that freedom. When we decided that, yes, we would like to catch some of those Peconic Bay weakfish while a few lilacs were still blooming, Chick, our friends Walter and Harry, and I set about planning one of our first fishing adventures. The key to the operation was the knowledge that we could get ourselves to Sag Harbor in Harry's old DeSoto.

We waited until after supper on what was a splendidly warm May evening. At Robertson & Zenger's hardware store, where we had bought our tackle, Archie Robertson had told us that weakfish were more likely to be active after dark—a bit of sound advice that still holds true. In Sag Harbor we rented a 16-foot sharpie with a five-horse Johnson on her stern and set out from a dock at the end of the town's Main Street. Standing on the end of that dock I could see Shelter Island and Orient Point farther to the northwest.

After a couple of pulls the motor started, and we were off on our own, the four of us in a boat at dusk on dark waters we had never before cruised. Now that's adventure.

We anchored not far from shore on the edge of the channel off North Haven; Archie had told us the weakfish was not a creature of deep waters. Our tackle was basic—no fly casters we, not in those days. We each had stiff, definitely well-used boat rods: stubby, all but inflexible, fitted with rugged, star-drag saltwater reels loaded with Cuttyhunk cotton line. Snelled hooks and pyramid-shaped lead sinkers designed to hold fast in swift tides made up our terminal gear.

Baiting up with strips of cut squid, we dropped our hooks to the bottom and waited, all of us certain our weakfish would arrive in a matter of minutes.

They did not, and never did. Even though we stayed until midnight, we caught only a few dogfish, skates, sea robins, spider crabs, and a sculpin or two. We laughed our way through the night, none of us upset that the weakfish weren't joining us. We were too exhilarated by our freedom, intoxicated with our approaching manhood.

Within a year Harry would join the Navy and train as an F4U pilot. Walter enlisted in the Marines and became a combat officer. Chick joined the Navy and ended up on a fighting ship off Okinawa. I flew 35 bombing missions over Europe aboard a B-17 Flying Fortress. We were, each of us, yanked out of boyhood a bit faster than we had anticipated.

Sitting in the warm September sun more than a half century later, I thought how fitting it was that I was still after weakfish, albeit in slightly different waters. Fishing has always been one of my life's holding points. But on this brief trip to Island Beach, the blustery cold front took command.

That old saw, "You should have been here yesterday," had seldom been as true as it was on this trip. Later that evening when we stopped by Bob Popovics's, he showed us some stunning film he'd shot the day before on the same beach where I had rested in the lee. Standing in the wash up to his ankles at the Atlantic's edge, Bob's viewfinder took in the sort of wild carnage that only schools of feeding fish create.

As packed masses of sea anchovies and peanut bunker swarmed into the shallows, they panicked and flung themselves in silver sprays high on the wet sand where they flopped and flickered like so many bright coins. Behind them, straight into the camera's eye, rushed large bluefish, weakfish, and albacore, tearing great gouts of white water from the sea's shining surface. It was total mayhem, so frenzied that fly casters tossing their Clousers and deceivers into the wash had them bitten off as often as they hooked up. As swarms of gulls screamed and circled in pale whirlwinds, the moment's ferocity gripped everyone: anglers, fish, bait, and birds.

It was a time for forgetting all else, even though Manhattan's towers rose just a few miles north. No wonder that young stockbroker sought surcease at New Jersey's Island Beach. It's a truly rare and splendid spot.

Tackle and Techniques

The status of today's weakfish population reminds me of needing a new fly line and by chance coming across just the one I wanted while rummaging through a drawer in my fly-tying desk. H.P. Rodman, founder of *Saltwater Sportsman* magazine, estimated in his 1948 book *The Saltwater Fisherman's Favorite Four* that weakfish were fished for by more anglers than striped bass, bluefish, and redfish combined. Yet by 1980 they were nearly nonexistent—the victims of nearly unregulated commercial fishing off the North Carolina coast. Although still on the mend, the weakfish population is vastly improved. In areas as far north as Long Island it's robust. What a delight it is to find these fish again available to inshore anglers. This past summer—for the first time in many years—a handful were caught in Buzzards Bay and on Martha's Vineyard. These areas represent the northern end of the weakfish's range, although they were once abundant there during the summer. Let's hope that the fisheries managers stick to their guns and give all anglers who live in—or are willing to travel to—the weakfish's historical range a chance to catch this great game fish.

Weakfish are not a fish that grows to the large sizes attained by most of the other species in this book. Although anecdotal evidence exists of 30-pounders, fish over 11 or 12 pounds are unusual. These larger fish are labeled tiderunners, and their maximum length is about 36 inches. The fish is handsome, possessing dark green and blue topsides, numerous small black spots, and lavender-tinged sides with a silvery white belly. The fin arrangement is similar to that of a striped bass but with a much longer second dorsal fin. The weakfish is a member of the croaker, or drum, family; the males of this species can push against their air bladder with their abdominal muscles, creating a croaking or drumming noise. The weakfish has a pair of prominent, canine-type teeth, or fangs, that help them grip and kill prey. These teeth are not, however, likely to cut your line like the mouth full of razor blades that a bluefish has.

Weakfish, also called squeteague and gray trout, migrate up the East Coast on a timetable that's quite similar to that of the bluefish, though they don't appear to have quite as much tolerance for cold water. In fact, weakfish trapped in shallow water during a cold snap, even as far south as North Carolina, may be killed. Like many of the game fish, once weakfish begin their migration they move quickly. Weakfish appear off the mouth of Chesapeake Bay in mid-April and historically arrived at Cape Cod from late April to mid-May. Most fish leave New England waters and Long Island Sound by early October. Fishing continues north of the Delaware Capes for another month, but coastal weakfishing is over by late November.

Although historically the weakfish spawned from Woods Hole south to the mid-Atlantic, the greatest concentration seems to be off the North Carolina coast. The weakfish like to spawn near shore and at the mouths of large estuaries; they are not, however, anadromous species and don't normally enter freshwater. One feature that aids the weakfish in its stock rebuilding is that both males and females become sexually mature as two- and three-year-olds. And they are fairly long lived, with fish of 30 inches and 10 pounds being over 10 years old.

The weakfish like shallow water. Although they are taken on the bottom by bait fishers, this often occurs inside shallow estuaries or right in the surf line, not far from the beach. Stretching almost to the horizon within Barnegat Bay are shorelines of marsh grasses, interlaced with tidal creeks, buffered from deep water by miles of shallow flats. The vast interlaced network of bays and marshes that lies behind the New Jersey barrier beaches is a superb place in which to find weakfish. Barnegat's warm, nutrient-laden shallows are home to a plethora of small marine creatures, nearly all of them food for the weakfish. Larger weakfish like larger bait, such as whole menhaden, and the smaller ones like other oily fin fish, especially spearing; the bay's grass shrimp and crab populations are also big draws (see figure 7.1). Barnegat is a rich nursery ground and just far enough south to hold weakfish during a long fishing season. Weak fishing has been an important sport fishery since times dating back to the oldest living memory and beyond. Van Campen Heilner, a saltwater fishing icon of the early middle part of the 20th century, wrote this paragraph about fishing for weakfish:

> Anyway, it's September, and we're down in the Barnegat Region, having just left the dock with our two live cars of shrimp (we don't use worms here) and are heading southward for the inlet. The big fleet of charter boats that were up in the Peconic region in May have left there and come down here with us. As we near the inlet we count over 200 boats, but they seem to be in long lines

like regiments of soldiers. As we draw closer we see this to be a fact; the boats are tied side by side, their sterns all in an even line, sometimes 15 or more in a group. This is called "lining up" for weaks.

Today's angler would fall over at the sight of so many boats, even in New Jersey. The population of the area was tiny in 1951 compared to today; they must all have been out weakfishing! It's incredible what good fishing will do to boost angler participation.

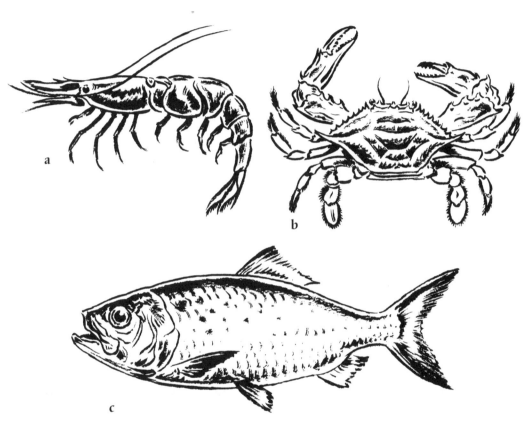

Figure 7.1   *Barnegat Bay's warm, shallow waters host huge populations of (a) grass shrimp, (b) blue claw crabs, and (c) menhaden.*

Heilner also talks about picking ranges by lining up old windmills on the shore. Those days are gone, and today you might line up on a factory and a power-generating plant, but the fish don't know that. Additionally, Island Beach State Park holds excellent frontage both on the bay and on the ocean. The inlet to Barnegat Bay passes through a pair of enormous jetties, the northernmost one being located at the south end of the park.

The action starts near Barnegat around the middle of May with the arrival of larger four- to seven-pound spawners. With the warmer water temperatures of June the smaller 12- to 18-inch weaks arrive in the bay. It's largely fish of the latter size that make up the summer-long fishery. John De Filippis, a local expert of long standing in the fly-fishing community says that the weaks move out of the bay starting with the full moon of October and are gone by early November. John says that migrating weaks follow the fall mullet run in mid-September along the ocean beaches. October and early November can provide excellent fishing on the beaches, especially at night. These fish, John feels, are probably migrants from the north, maybe Raritan Bay or Long Island Sound.

Island Beach State Park offers shorebound and small-boat anglers excellent access to weakfishing. From any of several paths and roads leading from the main access road, anglers can be walking the sod banks of the bay or paddling around in a canoe or kayak. A four-wheel-drive vehicle really helps on the front beach, but there are several walking accesses.

On the bay side the areas all along the sod banks can be productive, but points of land, areas where creeks are entering, or exceptionally steep drop-offs are prime holding grounds. Be careful wading here because you can step directly off a sod bank into water 10 feet deep. In some cases the banks are undercut and hold fish; walk lightly over the mushy sod banks so you don't spook fish holding there. During spring and fall, fishing can be good during the daytime, but during the heat of summer weakfishing is a dusk, dawn, or dark-of-night proposition. Don't kill a lot of time in one spot unless you're catching fish. Prospecting, or blind casting, is productive with a light-colored fly during daylight, or a black or black and purple fly at night. It's common at night to hear the pops of feeding weaks; the sound is crisper and less obtrusive than the tail slaps of feeding stripers. On calm evenings anglers listen keenly for this sound to locate schools of feeding fish. When you are shore fishing the bay, a southwest wind, which agitates the water along the sod banks, is best. Many strikes can come right up against the shore, especially at night, but it never hurts to lay out a good cast and cover some water. Here, up inside the bay, the incoming tide is best; near the inlet dropping water is favored, as it is in most inlet settings.

Although shore fishing can be productive, boat fishers have the best shot at making big catches of weakfish. Many anglers buy containers of live grass shrimp to use as chum. The shrimp are dribbled out by hand, a few tossed into the water as the last few disappear. Weakfish can sometimes be seen darting through the chum slick, and flies cast into this kind of action are usually effective.

Another approach to chumming that John De Filippis uses has some side benefits for the angler. First, John empties his crab traps and after enjoying a crab boil mashes up the shells and picked-over bodies. He then adds bunker oil to the brew and creates his crab chum. John ladles this chum into the water, which quickly attracts a good school of spearing. Weakfish then move in to feed on the spearing.

The most important part of chumming, according to John, is to select the right spot. The best locations are the confluences of channels within the bay, areas where creeks drain tidal flats, and sharp drop-offs along sod banks that signify deep water close to shore. If he's not chumming, John likes to drift through these areas watching his fish finder, looking for schools of weaks as he blind casts. By using a fish finder in this way, the angler who catches a fish can determine if it was a loner, in which case he should move on, or if it belonged to a school of weaks, in which case he should stick around.

Even the larger weakfish that you may catch at Barnegat do not require heavy equipment. Weaks do, however, put up a spirited fight, with a hard strike and plenty of thrashing on the surface. For most of the shore fishing five-weight through seven-weight rods should be adequate, unless it's blowing. If you need to pull a tiderunner back against the current from an anchored boat or if you're in the surf, an eight-weight rod or at the most a nine-weight rod will be adequate.

For shore casting, an intermediate line is perfect, while a sink-tip or sinking-head line may help from the boat, especially in moving water. The tapered leader that we mentioned in chapter 2 along with a 10-pound-test tippet will work fine. It would be smart to go up to 12- or 15-pound test in the surf because of abrasion in the wash. The beach at the park is a steep, ocean beach, complete with a well-developed outer bar. This kind of beach has a lot of nearshore structure, but a high backcast is necessary or you'll break the fly right off your tippet. Be cognizant of this or you'll spend time casting a fly with a broken point or no fly at all. Some of the points along the beach provide not only good structure but also a gentler slope, which gives you more room to backcast. Some fly fishers here cast almost parallel to the shore and do well because the weaks are often right in the wash. Both from the beach and off the bay side a stripping basket is necessary.

Many flies will work well on weakfish. The normal deceiver patterns in light colors will catch weaks that are patrolling for small baitfish; crab and shrimp patterns have their place here, too. Perhaps the most successful pattern is a chartreuse and white Clouser, as shown in figure 7.2. The weighted eyes of the Clouser cause it to hop up and down when stripped in; I think this really suggests to the predator the motion that a shrimp makes when swimming. A fin fish's whole body and tail undulate in a smooth, continuous motion. A shrimp, though, propels itself only by beats of its tail, and after every power stroke it must extend its tail against the resistance of the water. This method of propulsion is more erratic than that of a conventional fish. A Clouser, retrieved in short, frequent strips, may be an excellent simulation.

No one knows for certain where the name weakfish came from. Henry William Herbert, whom some call America's first outdoor writer, and who

FLY FISHING FOR SALTWATER'S FINEST

Figure 7.2 *Clouser fly.*

wrote under the pen name Frank Forester, offered a few possible explanations in his *Fish and Fishing,* published in 1855. Weak, thought Herbert, could be a phonetic corruption of the first five letters in squeteague, which is pronounced "squeat." Squeteague is the Indian name that New England settlers first heard the fish called by. Another possibility arises from a different nickname for the fish, which is wheatfish, possibly referring to the time of the wheat harvest as being good fishing. Finally some feel that it may be called the weakfish because it has a weak mouth compared with some other fish. Fly fishers can make no special preparation for dealing with the easily torn skin of the weakfish's mouth, but they probably don't need to anyway since the modest pressure of a fly rod is unlikely to rip the weakfish's mouth apart. When landing the fish, however, some care must be taken to avoid the fish's teeth. The weakfish's mouth is no place to put your thumb, as you might do with a striped bass. If you're wading, grabbing the fish firmly just in back of the head works fine, and if you're in a boat, a landing net is useful. Weakfish are excellent table fare, but they're very soft. It's important to eat this fish fresh and to ice it upon capture.

If you're interested in fishing from the shore at Island Beach State Park, a guide is probably not necessary. Park officials can point you in the direction of the shore access points, and maps are available at the office. If you're planning to fish out on Barnegat Bay, a day with a local guide is a good idea. Additionally, in the town of Seaside Park, right outside the park gates, several long-established tackle shops can give you good advice.

The Barnegat Bay area is not hard to find. The exit for Tom's River, exit 82 E from the Garden State Parkway, leads to a bridge over the bay that drops you off a few miles north of the park gate. I've stayed in the area a number of times myself, although I usually go after Labor Day brings an end to the summer season. Many off-season motels and several restaurants are available; rates are reasonable during the off-season. You should check with the park in advance if you are thinking of driving on the beach; permits are available for day, weekend, or annual periods.

For those who want to fish from a boat larger than a canoe, public launch ramps are found in most towns around the bay. If you're going to launch a

100

good-sized boat, it's wise to do it from the western shore of the bay and run across. There's a better selection of ramps, and you'll save time compared with driving out to Seaside Park. Barnegat Bay is not in itself big water, but it can kick up. Barnegat Inlet faces directly into the Atlantic; incoming waves, outgoing tides, and onshore winds can combine to create an impossible situation for even a good-sized boat.

New Jersey can be as cool as New England in the spring and fall. Off-season trips require the same clothing as a trip to Cape Cod or Montauk. Barnegat Bay is, however, considered to be mid-Atlantic, and in summer it can be hot and humid. On the bay side of Island Beach State Park in warm weather, the mosquitoes can be as large as the weakfish; bring bug dope.

Chapter 8

False Albacore—
Harkers Island,
North Carolina

*I*f the fates had chosen a slightly different course, I could have been a Banker. Not the lowercase banker that my parents would have been delighted to see me become (they would also have been happy to settle for lawyer) but a Banker with a capital B: the proud designation for the people of North Carolina's Outer Banks. Surely one of the nation's, and the world's, most singular coastal environments, the lacy stretch of wild barrier beaches that runs north from Cape Lookout to Knotts Island is a region unto itself. Like the place they have called home for more than two centuries, Bankers display a coastal culture of striking individuality, a people who have come to live with the sea as intimately as most of us walk our native land.

Before I ever set foot on one of those beaches I had a feeling for the place in my dreams. It began with flights along the Northeast Coast, south from Boston or New York City to Savannah, Charleston, or farther south to Florida's playgrounds. On clear days if I had a window seat I made certain I looked down whenever the plane's flight path took us just off the North Carolina coast. After Chesapeake Bay, a certain mark even from high altitudes, I would look hard for the arrow point of Albemarle Sound that drives deep into North Carolina's northernmost bulge. I'd be ready for the broader reaches of Pamlico Sound and the necklace of pale sand slivers that stretches so delicately between it and the open Atlantic.

In contrast to the rest of the earth, these slim barriers are deserted, lonely sweeps just a few miles from one of the planet's most populated urban and suburban complexes—the celebrated Northeast Corridor with its rich and powerful cities, its vast tangle of superhighways, its giant parking lots alongside an endless ramble of shopping malls. Yet on the state's outer edge there are these pale sweeps of beach, as pure as the sea itself. I would tell myself that if I could live anywhere, it would be on one of those beaches. In a moment the panorama would slip beyond the horizon, and the pilot's voice would tell me it wouldn't be long until we landed. But later, no matter what the excitement of the new, my mind's eye would return to those strands of sand, and I would ponder what it must be like to live in such elemental purity.

It could have happened, you know. My grandfather's father was born in North Carolina, and that grandfather, the father of my father, was a Methodist minister in Durham. He was also one of the founders of Trinity College, which became Duke University shortly after the Duke family gave Trinity the money that made the growth and transition possible. The Dukes were tobacco farmers who started a company called the American Tobacco Company, and it was through Trinity (later Duke) that the family knew my grandfather. He and my grandmother both died in late middle age, leaving nine children, of whom my father was the oldest. He was 19 and felt responsible for the continued support and well-being of his brothers and sisters.

His friend, Tony Duke, offered John Cole a job with American Tobacco. "No thanks," said my father, "I don't think too many folks are ever going to smoke those things." He was talking about cigarettes. Instead, my father headed out to New York City, a place he had heard defined as a land of opportunity, a place where he hoped to earn enough that he could send money home to his siblings in Durham. He paused on the way to teach one term of summer school at Woodberry Forest in Virginia, and that fall he arrived in Manhattan, where he lived for the rest of his years. He hadn't been there too long before he wrote his younger brother, telling him, "You better get up here, Henry. There's all kinds of rich Yankee women, and they just love Southern boys." This time, he was right.

But what if he had taken that job with American Tobacco? He would have stayed in North Carolina where I, his eldest son, would have been born. I would have spent my boyhood in Durham, or Winston-Salem, or Raleigh, one of the towns and cities where I still have cousins, distant though they be. And just as we children were blissfully sent off to Long Island's East End beaches during those blistering Manhattan summers, we almost as surely would have spent some time at a North Carolina summer cottage somewhere along the Crystal Coast, the name the state's promotional people have given to the seashores of eastern North Carolina.

You can bet that by the time I reached my early teens, I would have discovered Harkers Island. I was just 14 when inner impulses I have never questioned, nor fully understood, propelled me toward the creeks, ponds, salt marshes, and bays off Long Island's easternmost tip. First I sailed and swam and fished in Gardiners Bay with organized groups, designed to keep adolescents out of trouble by keeping them constantly in one summer class or another. But before that first summer was over, I launched my own un-supervised adventures. With my brother Chick and one or two equally adven-turous friends, we launched canoes in the ocean or pedaled our bikes 15 miles to Montauk and back to swim alone on secret beaches. I even made myself some wire eel pots and set a string of them in Georgica Pond. What's more, I learned to skin them so I could sell them to the village fish market.

By the time World War II had ended and I could take charge of my life, I left my city job and my rather raucous nightlife, moved to the end of Long Island, and became a commercial fisherman, the only occupation I knew that would be certain to keep me outdoors and on the water almost every day of the year, seven days a week. To help you understand the intensity of my compulsion, think about this: I was up most mornings at dawn, or be-fore, and I worked until long after dark for considerably less than the mini-mum wage. And I loved every minute of it! The men I fished with and worked with are some of the finest I have known in a long lifetime. They taught me honesty, stamina, and loyalty. It was through them that I was granted intimate and loving relationships with nature, the sea, and the ulti-mate integrity of an occupation so fundamental that it allows no corruptions, none.

These were discoveries I made myself, discoveries I earned in the face of opposition from my parents and my peers. In short, I had to fight to become a fisherman.

So what do you think would have become of me if I had lived in Winston-Salem instead of Manhattan? I would have found my way to the sea, that's what. In North Carolina, that means heading for the Outer Banks, where I would have worked alongside Bankers. And even though I knew in my heart of hearts that I could never become a genuine Banker, born into centuries of fishing tradition, I would have granted myself the indulgence of thinking of myself as one, although I would never say the word aloud.

Somewhere along the way, I would have discovered Harkers Island be-cause it is so pure, because it is an ultimate fishing community. Located at the very edge of the Atlantic, Harkers Island was, until just a couple of decades ago, isolated enough from our manic civilization that its culture attained a set of positive and humane values all but unknown to most Americans.

So if you're going to Harkers Island to cast a fly for albacore, and you should, or you're headed for any of the other fine fishing ports along the North Carolina coast, you will find it enriching to understand some of the history of the people and the place. This will add a fine and further dimen-sion of comprehension to your visit. There is still time, although not much, to learn something of these fishing people who have added so much to the national character, who have helped established the bedrock values the rest of us can build on.

Like the Bonackers of Long Island's East End and the Watermen of Chesapeake Bay's Eastern Shore, North Carolina's Bankers are descendants of some of the earliest English colonists, who settled the outermost coast because it was where they first arrived and where they knew they could subsist. They were already fishing people. England, after all, is an island, and many of the English who crossed the Atlantic in small sailing ships knew how to trap herring, hook cod, and harvest shellfish. Working south from Massachusetts, these true Yankees settled wherever bays, creeks, the salt marsh, and the open sea itself promised productive fishing grounds.

Harkers Island, like the rest of the Outer Banks, kept its promises from its whaling days of the 18th and 19th centuries to the mullet, oyster, crab, clam, scallop, and shrimp fisheries of the 20th. Because it is an island, and a small one at that, reachable only by small boat until the first bridge was opened on January 1, 1941, the character of its subsistence fishing and farming remained on a human scale well past the 20th century's midpoint. It was then, when commercial fishing along much of the nation's Atlantic coast began the transition from a low-tech, human-scale occupation to a high-tech, corporate-scale industry, that our seas were all but swept clean by the century's end.

Until the mid-1960s, the people of Harkers Island were truly insular, in the sense that while much of the rest of the nation rode the high waters of growth and technology, the Bankers were left in an eddy, revolving slowly in a place where the quiet customs and values of many generations prevailed. Some of the world's loveliest and most seaworthy wooden boats were built by island craftsmen, built by hand and eye, not computer or blueprint. These small boats were marked with the unique grace, rounded sterns, and flared bows that had been island traditions for centuries. If you visit, you can see them still, and in them you will recognize the curving hulls that today's manufacturers of mass-production fiberglass yachts have adopted as their own.

A fishing trip is what you make it, and in my opinion you miss a great deal if you fail to take the time and thought to understand the place. Yes, there are albacore galore in the waters off Harkers Island and the rest of the Outer Banks. And, yes, you will have a fine time with them on a fly rod. But at the end of the fishing day, the trip will become that much more memorable if you look around and understand something of where you are. In the case of Harkers Island, you are in a special place indeed. You are among people, fishing people, who have roots that reach far back in time, roots deep in an island that has been home to generations of Bankers.

"When I walk over the mounds of shells where my ancestors lived," says islander Susanne Yeomans Guthrie in the pages of the book *Island Born and Bred,* compiled by the Harkers Island United Methodist Women,

I can almost hear the children playing in the grass, the mothers sweeping the bare wood floors, and the fathers mending nets or opening clams in the backyard. A close look in the shells will often show a piece of bright blue or green plate or bowl. These fragments of history are gentle reminders, saying, "Don't forget your ancestors or their way of life." When I stop and think about that life, I can understand that it was not easy, it was not carefree, and it was not free from worry—but it was concerned, caring and loving. Everyone and everything existed together, not alone. The environment was not exploited or wasted: they only caught, killed, or used what they actually needed.

Consider these words written by Carmine Prioli, a professor of literature and folklore at North Carolina State University, where he has taught for 21 years. They are from the word-picture book, *Hope for a Good Season,* that he and photographer Ed Martin put together as a tribute to the vanishing way of life on Harkers Island.

The decline of commercial fishing on Harkers Island in the 1980s and 1990s has been accompanied by an increase in the numbers of tourists, summer vacationers and year-round recreational anglers. The influx of these visitors at times nearly doubles the population of about 1,600 for three or four months of the year. . . . Sound-side cottages rent for $700-$800 a week during the peak season and, of course, property values continue to climb along with tax rates, putting home ownership out of reach of the young island families. . . . What little sound-side property is available commands $1,000 per foot of waterfront. And half-acre parcels on property where Ebenezer Harker's home once stood can be had for $125,000 apiece.

Despite dismal financial prospects for those who choose to practice their traditional way of life, the toughest Bankers will continue to adapt. A few have turned to model boat building and decoy carving, trying to satisfy the insatiable demand from tourists for objects of coastal culture. Others will continue to build their own boats, set and repair their own crab pots and pound nets. They will work as long as there are fish and shellfish in the water and they are able-bodied enough to catch them. "We live from one season to the next," said Eddie Willis. "We hope! We hope for a good season and that takes you to the next one. . . . And so you live on hope more than you do on money."

It was only recently that the fall albacore blitz in the waters off the Outer Banks began to bring hundreds of fly fishers to North Carolina from October through November. More than any other East Coast location, these waters seem to attract larger albacore and many more of them. It's not unusual these days for even average fly fishers to hook and release 20 albies a day, with the smallest around 10 pounds and several topping out at 18. "You will," says a typical brochure (this one for the charter boat *Fritter),* "find acres of frenzied albacore smashing baitballs the size of basketball courts."

If you happen to be aboard the *Fritter,* take note of her flared bow. It echoes the lines of the lovely handcrafted wooden boats Harkers Islanders have been building for more than a century. Like so much on this small island and the breathtaking sweep of the Outer Banks, it resonates with the rich history of a pure and human-scale fishing community, the likes of which we will not see again. It's something to think about and learn more about when your great day's fishing comes to its end.

Tackle and Techniques

Years ago, I was leaning on the counter in Coop Gilkes's tackle shop on Martha's Vineyard. I had caught an albie earlier in the day that I had naively kept to eat—albies have very strong, dark flesh. I put the thing in the cooler, I told Coop, but it didn't fit very well, and when I tried to bend it, it wouldn't go. A striper or bluefish, I said, just conforms to the cooler, but the albie is firm as hell. "Yeah, albies," Coop said with reverence, "they don't conform to nothing."

Somehow, though, albies, or fat alberts as Harkers Island folks call them, aren't quite as regaling or exotic as bonito. Maybe it's because, unlike the bonito, they often show up in such enormous schools that they're easier to take for granted. But the false albacore, or little tunny, is perhaps the fastest, strongest inshore saltwater fly-fishing quarry that exists. Their attributes are not lost on the saltwater fly-rodding community. Modeled after the larger tunas, the albies look like their miniatures and fight the same way. I've hooked albies of only 10 or 12 pounds in shallow water near the beach and have had to start the motor and pursue them just to keep them from stripping 200 yards of backing from a reel with a very firm drag.

Albies look similar to bonito but are much stouter forward, and it's not fat that's wrapped around those shoulders. The quickest way to tell the two apart is by the shape of the dorsal fins. The bonito has a long, low dorsal that extends all along the upper back. The albie has what looks like a mast and sail for its dorsal. Its base runs only a short distance along the back; a long gap exists between it and the anterior dorsal (see figure 8.1). The bonito has broad and distinct stripes that run the length of its body; these are lacking on an albie, which has instead dark, troutlike vermiculations all along its upper back. While leaping from the water, both fish appear green and silvery, and it's almost impossible to tell one from the other.

False albacore are a fish of the southern oceans; the south side of Cape Cod is the extreme northern edge of their range. They come inshore north of Cape Hatteras during only the warmer periods of the summer, typically showing up off Montauk in late August as seasonal water temperatures hit their peak. Their powerful physiques, their habit of leaping from the water's surface in pursuit of bait, and their fondness for flies make them sought after during their brief visits off the Northeast Coast. False albacore fishing, although different from true sight fishing, as on the tropical flats, is still visual fishing. The

Figure 8.1 *The easiest way to tell albies from bonito is by their dorsal fins.*

feeding albies, sometimes in large schools, tear the water's surface into sheets of spray and violent whirlpools—caused by their powerful tails—often during the sunniest parts of the day. My guide friends tell me that even experienced anglers can be badly rattled by the sight of an oncoming school of leaping albies.

The south side of the Carolina Cape's Point Lookout area is the foremost location for fly-rod fishing for false albacore on the East Coast. Although the appearance of albies in this area is nothing new, the attention now being focused on the area is a phenomenon of recent years. As recently as the early 1990s this fishery was largely undiscovered by the saltwater fly-fishing community. After a local fly rodder showed this spot to some of the industry's top personalities—who then did a television show on the fishery—the word really got out. In recent falls, a gathering of many of the most serious saltwater fly rodders from around the country has taken place on Harkers Island. It has taken an exceptional fishery to bring so many excellent anglers to one spot during such a narrow window of time. The large run of exceptionally big fat alberts is the greatest part of the reason. But it's also that the Carolina Capes are the last outpost of a northern fishery, the most distant fishing location that can be considered a sane drive from the mid-Atlantic and Northeast population centers. The Cape Lookout albie fishery gives these anglers a crack at this popular game fish after they've left their local waters, but they're bigger and more numerous than the fish that people who live north of Hatteras are used to seeing.

The Pasfield family owns the Harkers Island Fishing Center—a complex of marina, fishing store, and motel. After Rob Sr. retired from the marine trades industry in the Northeast, the family—including Rob Jr., who was at one time the mate of famous shark-fishing wildman Capt. Frank Mundus of Montauk—ended an East Coast search for a marina by buying this facility. Rob Jr. quickly realized the potential of the false albacore fishery. He now guides and handles the bookings for six other local guides; while openings still exist, everyone is busy. Additionally, Rob has made arrangements with a hotel in nearby Beaufort should additional accommodations be needed. Rob ably guided me around the albie grounds and revealed the local techniques.

Cape Lookout is the southernmost part of North Carolina's famous Outer Banks—a 250-mile stretch of sand beaches that enclose massive bays between themselves and the mainland. It's the northernmost point that I've heard of that constantly holds at least a few albies from late April right through to early December. The Gulf Stream here is only 35 miles offshore, and offshore anglers report false albacore to be present there during the winter months. Rob even mentioned catching some albies in the late summer that were well under a foot in length; these must be young-of-the-year false albacore. The best albie fishing develops when water temperatures drop to the low 60s and high 50s, temperatures well off their summer highs.

What's remarkable about this fishery, though, is the number of albies that are present and the great sizes they attain. I've seen some pretty fair surface blitzes around Montauk, and every now and then someone catches a 17- or 18-pounder there, but albies that size are as scarce as hen's teeth. At Harkers Island, however, I photographed several acres of large albies herding brown balls of bay anchovies on the surface of the water. There was no room in the melee for one more albie, nor in the air for one more seagull. At the height of the activity you couldn't think of casting into the center of the fish because hooking a bird was a certainty. Fat alberts of more than 20 pounds are caught regularly, with fish over 15 pounds a daily occurrence during the season's peak.

The Cape Lookout area excels for albies because of the rich food system provided by the vast network of Core and Bogue Sounds, the Newport and North Rivers, and the Intracoastal Waterway running down from the Neuse River just to the north. All this bait is swept out through two nearby inlets: Beaufort and Borden. Borden Inlet enters directly into a protected bay, filled with current, that's around two miles wide, called Cape Lookout Bite. The bite is the area's premier spot because it can hold many boats and because its nearly circular shape allows fly fishing on calm seas during the brisk winds of late autumn. Beaufort Inlet is a much wider channel that runs straight out into the ocean. Albies can be anywhere near the inlet, and when surface action slows, many anglers chum for the albies that seem to be constantly available there.

For anglers who prefer to wade, the area provides some of the better shore-fishing possibilities that exist for false albacore. Beaufort Inlet's western side can be accessed at Fort Macon State Park, which provides parking 150 yards from a jetty that can produce on either tide. There is also regular ferry service from Beaufort to Shackleford Banks, where anglers can wade an extensive, structure-laden sand beach on the east side of the inlet, also a productive location.

Cape Lookout can be accessed by ferry from Harkers Island. A four-wheel-drive vehicle allows anglers to fish the surf of Cape Point's sandy tip and the shallow flats on its west side. We saw many big albies running around in two feet of water on those flats. The ferry will also drop you off at another sand spit that forms the western end of Cape Lookout Bite. Terrific current flows by this point, especially on the ebb tide, and this may be the best location of all. Be careful wading here, though, because like all current-swept sand spits it has some sheer drop-offs.

A boat, however, provides the best access to this fishery. We saw boats ranging in size from 16-foot aluminums up to high-20-foot center consoles. One guide, staying at the Harkers Island Fishing Center, had dragged his 27-footer down from the Nantucket waters that he fished during the summer. Many days in fall produce strong winds and choppy waters. I would want at least a 20-foot semivee hull under me, and preferably a deep vee.

The best fishing comes from four locations: the waters in and around Beaufort and Borden's Inlets, the broad stretch of ocean off Shackleford Banks, and the waters around Cape Point. Anglers locate the fish either by seeing them breaking on the surface or by locating birds that are sitting on the water or flying around obviously patrolling a piece of water. Birds in the air can see much deeper into the water than we can. They will dog the schools of predators until the fish push bait to the surface and into their reach. Still another method of finding feeding albies is to follow the working shrimp boats. The shrimp boats drag their nets behind them, catching both shrimp and a wide variety of baby fish. After the net is hauled back, the fishers sort the shrimp from the "by-catch" and shovel the by-catch overboard. The gulls—which always follow these boats, allowing them to be easily spotted—go berserk when the by-catch is discarded, and the albies follow in the boat's wake eating what the gulls miss. Sometimes you can see the albies boiling in the wake; more often you blind cast while using your depth finder to locate the fish.

Albies feeding on the surface are the pickiest. Up in the water column, where their vision is the most acute, you may have to match carefully at least the size of the prey. The information that we presented in the bonito chapter covers this fully. One difference, though, is that the albies seem less leader shy. As with bonito, the best presentation is one in which you drop the fly in front of the feeding fish and retrieve it away from them, mimicking the actions of a real baitfish. If you can get in front of the school and make your cast as they approach—don't be afraid to cast well in advance and let your fly sink a bit until they get near—and then start stripping it as the fish visibly reach your fly, you'll rarely miss.

You'll be all set if you have a selection of bonito flies—epoxies, 3-Ds, Clousers, deceivers—to imitate bay anchovies and peanut bunker (see figure 8.2). The common colors of white, olive, and chartreuse are appropriate. The only difference is that you'll want them all tied on stout hooks. Stay away from tiny, thin-wire hooks here. I also like hooks that have a deep pocket, like the Mustad 7766—although there are many others that fit the description—in a size of at least 1/0. Albies are strong, and at Harkers Island you're likely to end up pulling on a lot of big ones. Wimpy hooks will simply bend open under the pressure.

Figure 8.2 *Epoxy silverside fly.*

If the fish aren't feeding on the surface the guides will chum in likely areas. The Harkers Island Fishing Center sells packages of frozen bay anchovies to use as chum. The technique is neither messy nor difficult, and in my view it's perfectly sporting. The block of frozen baitfish is placed in a bucket of seawater where it slowly thaws. The chummer simply picks individual baitfish from the surface of the block and tosses one into the water as the previous one disappears. It's hard to imagine that such a diminutive stream of chum could attract the albies, but it sure does. Some days, after chumming for a short while, the fishing becomes a nearly every-cast affair. Pulling on one mega-albie after another for a few hours has left more than one angler unable to come out again the next day. I found the fish in the chum line more than willing to take nearly anything for a fly.

When it comes to tackle requirements, rugged is the word. Albies exposed to too long a fight are often tough to revive. You need a rod that has enough backbone to end the fight relatively quickly; a 10-weight rod with a stiff butt section is about right. One of the modern cannons that have a fast action is helpful in driving casts into the normally windy conditions. Your reel must have a solid drag system, and it should hold at least 200 yards of backing. Many reels filled with even this amount of 30-pound-test backing will be nearly emptied by a big albie that has been hooked in the shallow water along the beach. The retrieve speed on such a reel is reduced to nearly nothing; you can't possibly keep up with an albie who decides to run just as far in the opposite direction as he already has in the first. This is a fishery where the large wide-arbor reels, filled with Spectra backing, are what you need. I also suggest two outfits: one equipped with an intermediate line for surface fishing and one with a 300- to 350-grain sinking head for fishing in the chum.

Surprisingly, anglers use some very heavy tippets on these fish. I suggest having some of the tapered leaders that we discussed back in chapter 2 with tippets down to 15-pound test; albies feeding in clear, shallow water and on fine bait may be a bit too fussy for anything heavier. But many at Harkers Island use 20- or even 30-pound-test tippets to control big albies quickly; this is especially appropriate in an area where several boats are chumming near one another over a school of fish. But "control quickly" is a relative term; I asked Rob if the anglers using 30 could simply stop a 15-pound albie in its tracks. Hell no, said Rob, something's going to give. Often it's the rod, especially in the hands of those unfamiliar with the proper rod angle to fight a strong fish. Back at the shop, Rob Sr. showed me a famous-maker rod that had literally exploded when an angler tried to stop a big albie from diving under the boat. The rod had broken in several places, including right in the middle of the foregrip. I can't stress enough that on strong fish, including albies of just 15 pounds, you must keep the rod angle low compared to the direction of the pull; you must use the butt of the rod.

Despite their strength and incredible speed, albies are not tough to land. A hook easily penetrates the mouth, and it usually holds. They have no teeth that can cut your line, and they never jump once hooked. Typically an albie will head for the horizon the second it's hooked. After a quick pull to set the hook, all attention should go to clearing the line, because virtually all albies make it to the reel, most very quickly. After one or two long runs—sometimes in opposite directions—the albies will lie on their sides and swim in circles. This fighting style is common with virtually all members of the tuna and mackerel families; it is the time when most rods are broken by those who try to lift too hard, with too high a rod angle. Take a tip from the stand-up big-game anglers; move the fish in short, rapid strokes and lift it only a few inches at a time, but often. Once at boatside, albies are usually tired and not evasive. They have a rigid, sickle-shaped tail that makes a perfect handle for tailing. Using a large net allows you to land them even quicker, and without getting wet.

Harkers Island is approximately two hours from Interstate 95—use U.S. Route 70 east—and just under three hours from the Raleigh-Durham airport, the closest large airport and one with car rentals.

Although in summertime North Carolina is a hot place, in the late fall it can be nearly as cool as New England. I'd suggest the same clothes that we did for Martha's Vineyard or Montauk. Because it's windy almost every day at this time of the year, foul-weather gear is a requirement. You'll be looking at an ocean surface often covered by blinding reflections caused by a low sun angle, so quality polarized sunglasses are a must. A warm pair of gloves is a great luxury as you move between fishing spots.

Chapter

9

Permit and Bonefish— Islamorada, Florida

According to the International Game Fish Association, each of the five tippet-class, world-record permit taken on a fly have been caught within a few miles of Key West. This is close to irrefutable evidence that there are no finer permit fishing grounds on the globe. Well, if there are, they are still waiting to be discovered.

When one of my life's several anomalies moved me from Maine to Florida's Key West in 1986, I scarcely knew what a permit was. I surely didn't know what one looked like, nor did I have any idea of their enchanted identity in the eyes of serious fly fishers. But if you are nuts about fishing, as I am, and you hang around anglers in Key West for a few years, as I did, you will hear many permit stories. I have heard thousands, and I'm certain there are thousands more that somehow got by me. This much I have learned: permit stories are much easier to come by than the fish in person.

Key West is a fine jumping-off spot for your quest. The two-by-three-mile coral blip is a resort in every sense of the word. It has more bars, more tacky souvenir shops, more hotels and motels, more restaurants, and fewer swimmable beaches than any comparable spot in the entire, overrun state of Florida. But this grossly overpopulated, semitropical, southernmost dot at the end of U.S. Route 1 has something no other town or city in the nation can claim: it is surrounded by the world's most exciting saltwater fly-fishing waters. And the permit is the most elusive, the most exciting, fish that swims in those fascinating waters.

I watched one morning from my skiff as a permit rose from beneath Key West Harbor's main channel, less than a half mile from Sloppy Joe's notorious watering hole on Duval Street. The permit began chomping on the silver-dollar-size green crabs that rode on top of a yellow gold raft of floating seaweed about the size and shape of a large manhole cover. I was within shouting distance of several hundred thousand T-shirted tourists, yet here was this wariest and wildest of sea creatures not 30 feet from me picking off breakfast snacks like a kid eating crackerjacks. That's a distance even a poor fly caster could manage, and that was a happy fish, believe me.

Of course, by the time I collected myself, yanked my fly rod from its place under the gunwale and found a fly that came somewhere close to being fit for a permit, the great fish was gone. I can, however, still see its round, perfect, ebony eye—looking as large as a jet-black tennis ball—staring at me as I killed the outboard and drifted toward it. "I know you're there, you jerk," that permit seemed to say, "and I know you can't get yourself together until long after I've swallowed the last of these crabs. So why not just forget about me, and go on and have a nice day."

This is not difficult to do if you're afloat on the waters off the Keys, for this is a unique and wild environment that must be experienced to be believed. From Key West it's 120 or so miles east to Key Largo and the causeway to the Florida mainland. That's as the crow flies. But in a 16- or 18-foot flats skiff there are enough miles of shoal water to contain places still so secret they have yet to be fished, even though the number of anglers drawn to these exotic, wild, and fertile waters increases each year.

Flying above this intricate embroidery of mangrove hummocks, twisting channels, vast expanses of knee-deep flats (and that's at high tide), and aquamarine pools is about the only way you can begin to comprehend the scale of this marvelous watery wilderness. The place is too complex, too much of a twisting, turning maze, to be realized from the surface of its green, silver, and azure waters. Even as you fly above it, you are in danger of becoming disoriented, so intricate are the random patterns stitched over the millennia by tides, trade winds, and hurricanes.

The place itself is reason enough to fish the Keys. This is the world's largest marine sanctuary, its waters protected and proclaimed forever wild by both state and federal statute. Like the Everglades a few miles north, the vast expanse of flats, coral heads, channels, basins, and countless keys (some no larger than a cabin cruiser) is a place protected. Channels and passes exist where no engine-powered watercraft can venture. There are places where the unwary and unwise will find themselves hopelessly lost, in spite of sophisticated electronics and computer chips.

There is no such thing as a dull day on the water when you fish the Keys. There is simply too much going on around you. Pelicans and frigate birds soar; the great, dark shapes of giant rays glide past, the pale edges of their white undersides rippling; silver showers of tiny baitfish erupt from below in luminous fountains; great sharks arrive from nowhere, a menace alongside your skiff for one long, sudden moment before they vanish. But now you know they are out there, just as you know that barracuda are lying still as emerald logs and great white herons are staked out like fence posts across a flat that shimmers like a desert mirage under a majestic midday sun.

An eternal mystery abides in these thousands of square miles of warm and shallow waters that embrace the Keys' north side, a mystery that will remain unsolved forever. There are more still farther west of Key West, 25 miles or more across Boca Grande Channel to the Marquesas and from there to the Tortugas and beyond. If you lived a thousand years and cruised these waters each day of your long life, there would still be places beyond your ken. And if you never hooked a single fish of the millions you might find, each day and each night of those thousand years would be unforgettable.

But making contact with those fish, connecting along the electric fibers of a fly line, makes any day or night that much more memorable. As you will hear from the few anglers who have hooked a permit, there are few comparable angling experiences the world around.

My friends Nathaniel Pryor Reed and Capt. Gil Drake are one of the top permit pairs of the past half century. Along with Del Brown, who holds three of the five fly-rod records, and Bill Levy, a permit pioneer who created the original epoxy permit flies, Nat and Gil have met and enticed more permit than most of us will ever see (not including Del Brown of Islamorada, who fishes permit more than 100 days each year). When last I checked, Nat (who is well into a sturdy middle age) had taken his 41st permit on a fly (of which more later), and by this time I'm sure that number has increased. But he is not an angler after world records: he fishes a barbless hook and will break off any fish he suspects is dangerously near total exhaustion.

Yet Nat could not have established his remarkable record without Gil. Between them, they are a rare combination of permit talents. Gil knows the tides, the winds, the flats, the water temperatures, the diurnal and lunar rhythms, and an indefinable range of intangibles that give him a permit-locating edge. Over the years of his meticulous record keeping and the knowledge assembled during thousands of days on those mysterious shoal waters that surround the Keys, he has developed an exceptional sense of fish. He leaves the dock each early morning with more confidence than most of us will ever realize. And more often than any mortal I know or have word of, Gil finds permit. His skills are that rare combination of extrasensory perception and diligent attention to every aspect of the watery world he navigates.

Those skills are not wasted on Nat, a superb caster of flies, especially permit flies and especially in the windy weather that favors those who quest after this wary fish. Not easily taken in any weather, permit are all but impossible to fool when the air is still and the water's surface is smooth. No, unfortunately for most of us average fly casters, permit are more approachable when it's windy. Not only does the wind invigorate the fish, it creates riffles of windblown water that make it more difficult for this fish's huge, black eyes to spot a stalking angler.

As you might expect, both Nat and Gil pray for wind whenever they pursue permit, a challenging quest that is as much a hunt as it is a fishing expedition. Permit must be sighted and successfully stalked before a single fly is cast. This is the essence of flats fishing, the added dimension that sets it apart.

Nat Reed has kept an angling journal for more than 20 years. It is more than a delightful diary written to enjoy long years after those bright-water days are memories; it is also a meticulous record of wind, weather, time, place, and tide—data that can help compute where and when this elusive creature is most likely to be found. So consider this entry from the 1997 Fishing Log of Nathaniel Pryor Reed III. If you are questing after permit, there is much here you can learn.

> Breakfasted at Pepe's [Nat opens with a splendid recommendation] and then to the marina where Gil, his flats skiff, and the tide were waiting and off we went.
> We started at Mullet Key with limited visibility and a 12- to 15-mph east-southeast wind. The tide flowed in and at 9:30 A.M. we spotted our first permit

close in. I rolled a merkin [of which more later] to him, hit him on the nose and he vanished.

Then I saw another something. "Gil, what's that big, dark shape out there at 3 o'clock?"

"Nat, that's a big permit. Go for it!"

Gil turned the skiff, giving me a perfect shot. The Reed children's gift of a nine-foot, 10-weight Thomas & Thomas rod delivered the fly a foot in front of the permit who dashed up, tailed on the fly, and spooked!

An hour later, a similar sighting, a similar cast, exactly the same reaction. "Gil, let's try a new merkin. They don't like this one."

The wind began to gust to 20 mph or more. A few minutes later, a nice, round 18-pounder rushed four feet to a poorly cast fly, tailed on it, came tight for an instant, and was gone. It is so rare an opportunity to have a permit take a fly that it is a sickening feeling to have blown an opportunity.

We had not fully regained our humor when a 12-pounder came into view. Good cast. He tailed on the fly but spooked when I bounced it once. I looked at Gil in desperation. He shrugged and repeated the permit guide's credo: "It's not why they do not take a fly; it's why do they take the fly."

Then Gil spotted a permit a fair way out and expertly poled the skiff toward it. My first cast was short. "Pick it up and try again," said Gil. "This time, hit him on the nose." I followed the Boss' directions. The permit flushed, raced toward the skiff, then suddenly turned and raced back to where the fly had fallen. Without hesitation, it seized the fly and I landed it after a wonderful, long running battle: 17 pounds of golden permit. My 41st! The tide banked; Gil and I sat down and collected our wobbly legs.

We moved to Northwest Channel and staked out for lunch, then spotted a mid-sized permit feeding off the bow. Gil, sandwich in hand, turned the skiff with the other, giving me a perfect shot. The fly hit the fish on the nose. It stopped, watched the merkin sink, tailed on it, stared, then stared some more, and then departed.

As the afternoon wore on, a cold, windy front moved in. Ours had been the morning of 1997. We never had as many permit come to the fly with such interest. With any kind of luck, it could have been a three- to five-fish morning. But that's the February gamble. Some of the largest permit are seen on the flats in February if the weather is mild and moderately calm. I'm ready to gamble again next year and the year after that! For the permit remains the fish of dreams—the most difficult of all the shallow water fish to stalk and catch. Permit are the quest and goal of the angler who is satisfied with his catches of tarpon, bonefish, and all other trophies of the saltwater flats.

Now, as promised earlier, let's hear a few words on the merkin, the permit angler's favorite fly (see figure 9.1). This explanation comes courtesy of Capt. Jeffrey Cardenas, currently the proprietor of The Saltwater Angler, the Keys' finest fly and tackle shop, and formerly one of the Keys' finest guides. He is the author of the best-selling book *Marquesa—A Time and Place With Fish*, from which the following is excerpted.

"To the uninitiated," writes Jeffrey, aboard his houseboat, the *Huck Finn*, moored in the Marquesas' Mooney Harbor, a permit is a fish looking much like a pompano, which, in turn, looks much like the lid of a frying pan with a couple of eyes and fins stuck on it. The permit I watch this morning are the size of garbage can lids. They live offshore, but come onto the flats to feed. A 20-pound permit has an eye larger that that of a 200-pound man. This eyesight, combined with an enhanced lateral line, makes their sensory apparatus absolutely electric.

My presence 250 feet away has already made them nervous. Right now I'm thinking about trying to fool these fish with an outrageous fly made of feathers and yarn and blue rubber legs. It's supposed to be a crab imitation. The body is made of Aunt Lydia's rug yarn. Lead eyes make it dive like a crab and the rubber legs help it dance.

The pattern was designed by the world's most successful permit fisherman, a California angler named Del Brown and his Key West fishing guide Jan Isley. It's called a merkin, which, loosely translated, is a medieval term for a pubic wig.

In the Middle Ages when a woman of ill repute was known to carry lice or disease, public health officials would order her pubic hair shaved to announce her condition to potential customers. To be able to continue her occupation despite this exposure, an ambitious woman would visit her local merkin maker to be fitted with a hairpiece that would supposedly fool her John in their hour of darkness.

And thus the merkin. When else in history but the Middle Ages would there have been a need for a pubic wig? And when else but the 1990s would there be a permit fly named after it?

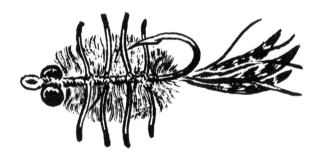

Figure 9.1　*Merkin fly.*

Who else but Capt. Cardenas would offer such an entertaining bit of permit-fishing lore?

Years before he wrote his fine book, I was fishing with Jeffrey when the unexpected happened. We were staked out in his Maverick flats skiff on the oceanside edge of the Seven Sisters, a string of seven channels that cuts through a long flat east of Woman Key. Tarpon, which is what we were after, navigate those channels and often cruise the flats when the tide rises. We had seen a few; I jumped one that broke off in a matter of split seconds, and after that we stopped for lunch. Jeffrey, I'm certain, was not just hungry; he hoped the pause might cure my casting screw-ups.

He sat high on the poling platform, ever observant while I munched on one of Jean's masterpiece cold chicken sandwiches. I had it about half gone when Jeffrey yelled, "Permit! Three fish. Two o'clock. Headed our way. Get up there on the bow. Get up there and cast!"

So I did but far from adroitly. I did see the permit: lovely dark and silver shapes against the pale sand. And I did cast in their general direction. The fly was a large Brown Cockroach, a tarpon fly. I cast short of the fish, but they were still moving quite casually in our direction, closing in on the fly.

As so often happens with me, I got the fly line looped around my reel. During the time it took me to put it right, the permit moved within a foot of the fly, now at rest on the marl. As I straightened my tangle, I twitched the fly line and the fly, which was just what the lead permit wanted.

"He's eating it! He's eating it!" yelled Jeffrey. "Now, strike him!"

I lifted the rod tip, felt pressure, and pressed back—not a proper strike. But lucky, really lucky.

"He's on! He's on!" Jeffrey yelled, as unbelieving as I.

That was a tough fish. He made splendid, strong runs. With Jeffrey yelling instructions in my ear every five seconds or so, after 20 minutes I had the permit at the boat.

Jeffrey had it in his net and on board in seconds. Then came the verifying photo, and we released the fish, healthy and perhaps wiser.

Jeffrey slapped me on the back, hard. "Wow! A permit on a fly. You got a permit on a fly!"

"Yeah," I said. "Nothing much to it."

Because one always remembers such moments, I can tell you it was a 23-pound permit caught aboard the *Waterlight* with Capt. Jeffrey Cardenas around noon on May 24, 1989. I still have 40 to go to catch up with Nat Reed.

As for bonefish, well, as far as I'm concerned I'll never catch up. That's not because I haven't had a bunch of chances. I think it's my own, special, one-of-a-kind angling jinx. Somewhere far back in time one of my ancestors must have committed some unspeakable crime against bonefish, and all his descendants and I are paying a terrible price.

This is not to imply that the Keys are not good bonefish grounds: they are indeed. Success with bonefish, however, increases the farther west and north you travel from Key West. The largest school of bonefish I have seen was on a flat about 30 minutes north of Islamorada. Of course, I cast to them and, of course, they ignored my fly.

I say of course because that refusal was in keeping with every prior and subsequent (except one) bonefish encounter, and there have been many. I have learned this much, however: your best bet for the largest bonefish, especially in winter, is on the east side of Elliott Key in Biscayne Bay. Yes, just a few minutes south of Miami, a city no longer associated with excellent angling in the minds of most Americans.

This is not to say you won't find bonefish in the Keys. You will. Given that you are not me, you will most likely find one that will eat your fly. Many anglers have.

I'm just not one of them, although it's not as if I haven't been warned. Try a quarter century ago on one of my early visits to the Keys and south Florida. Thanks to an invitation many anglers would have done almost anything to wrangle, I stood on the bow casting platform of a flats skiff being expertly poled along the east shore of Elliott Key. Given my guide's reputation, I expected to see the slim, silvery, ghostly shadows of cruising bonefish almost everywhere I looked across the pale flats. But as the day began to dwindle, so did those foolish fantasies. My attention span sagged almost as much as my weary legs. Just as I was about to request a 10-minute break, the captain called, "Five bones at one o'clock, about two casts out. Get ready!"

"Bones at two o'clock. They're happy fish. Do you have them yet?"

"No."

"Three o'clock now. In range! In range! Cast. Cast now!"

I waved the rod, false casting. I still hadn't seen those bonefish. But I kept waving the rod. I heard heavy footsteps thumping. Within seconds I had company.

Suddenly at my side, the captain yanked the rod from my hands. With a mighty back cast, a double haul, and a cast that seemed to soar forever, he dropped a Crazy Charlie a foot in front of the lead bonefish.

Whereupon the fish ate the fly. The captain struck the fish, then shoved the rod back into my hands.

"Reel," he said. "You got him."

So I stood there as that fine fish ripped off 100 feet or so of backing; then I followed through with the fundamentals. After 10 minutes or so, I saw my first bonefish. It was at the end of my leader, perhaps 30 feet from the boat, making a spirited fight for its freedom. "Ah, so that's what they look like," I told myself as I tried not to lose the fish. Something told me that if I did my captain might be seriously upset.

But he was at my side with a net as the bonefish neared the skiff. Netting the trophy gently, he handed me the net, told me how to hold the bonefish, snapped a photograph and then released the fish, which seemed none the worse for our encounter. A week later when the prints arrived at our Maine home I took them to the office and walked them around from one work-station to the next. "That's my bonefish," I bragged, and after delivering that lie over and over, I had almost come to believe it.

Some 10 years later, I was beginning to think I could set things to rights by casting to, hooking, and landing a bonefish all on my own. After all, it was October and I was fishing with Jeffrey, one of the best there ever was.

Aboard his *Waterlight* we headed east out of Key West toward the backcountry's vast expanse of hummocks, keys, channels, flats, and sudden pools of luminous emerald that hold watery secrets in their darkening depths. Past the Mud Keys and on to the cluster of hummocks just north of the Snipe Keys we raced until Jeffrey, arriving at a place only he knew, shut down the outboard and began poling a narrow, curling flat at the edge of the Gulf.

He must have had those bonefish trained. Easing us around the corner of a hummock, he called out, "Two bonefish, ten o'clock. They're close. Cast now!"

Cast I did, rather well, I thought, as my second backcast whistled by and I leaned into the final forward pull, watching the fish to see where my fly might land. I never saw it. But I surely felt it as it slapped me smartly between my thinly clad shoulder blades. Whap! That fly stung like a wasp.

Experienced fly-fishing guides have seen it all. If they are to survive their careers with sound minds and unbroken spirits, they learn not to get emotionally involved with their anglers or the infinite number of ways those anglers can screw up a perfect opportunity. Nevertheless, there was just a hint of bristle in Jeffrey's voice as he called down from his poling platform. "OK. OK. Those fish haven't moved. Pick up and try again."

And so I did. But in my shame and haste, I managed to get a good portion of my fly line pinned under my right foot. This time, the cast looked splendid until the line fetched up and the fly hit the water about 15 feet short of those remarkably placid bonefish. They must have known they had nothing to fear.

By the time I'd regrouped, the skiff had drifted a few feet closer and those bones decided they'd hung around long enough. With barely a flicker of their translucent tails, the two silver wraiths rocketed north toward the Gulf's deep sanctuary and vanished. Gone. Only a faint roil of the bottom's coral dust told us they had indeed been there, waiting for me all morning long.

Over the years that followed, Jeffrey kept trying. He began a gentle teasing technique designed to help me break the bonefish barrier, which led to an early-morning adventure on a flat near the Marvin Keys Channel, some three channels east of Jewfish Basin.

With his skiff securely staked, Jeffrey began wading south, following the channel's edge. As he left, he told me I occupied the most likely spot.

"Wade across here," he said, pointing, "and watch the Gulf side of the flat. The bonefish will move in with the tide and come across here."

Yes, I thought, and angels will swoop down to carry me to triumph. I slipped reluctantly over the gunwale and began wading. That wonderfully warm water eased past my calves, soaking the bottom three inches of my cotton shorts. I don't really like wading the mushy, fertile flats. I never have. I'm too conscious of the creatures that share that murky space. Stories of stingrays who bury their barbed and toxic spines deep in the shins of unwary anglers, and the subsequent bloody removal process, perhaps blood poisoning and hospitalization. Those images travel with me whenever I wade, imagining catastrophes that will cause hysteria, intense pain, and most likely an early and ignoble death. So I do not wade, I shuffle, hoping that whatever peril lies buried in my path will take proper alarm and vacate.

So shuffle I did. I got as far as 15 feet from the skiff then turned and wished I was back aboard her as she sat swinging there in the gentle tide, a sure and certain sanctuary. As I stood there cloaked in misery, a school of bonefish, perhaps a dozen or more, swung in from the Gulf and glided onto the flat, headed my way at a moderate cruising speed. A 30-foot cast would have dropped my pink-shrimp fly right on their noses.

Ah, it could have been classic. Those bonefish played their fabled role to perfection—silvery ghosts soaring like shadows across the green waters and creamy flats. But then came another shadow, this one off on my other side, much larger, moving more slowly than the bonefish but with much more stubborn intent, and headed straight for me.

Shark! Of that I was certain. I had seen too many in these waters to be mistaken. But what species I knew not. I was too low in the water to get a good look at the shark's distinguishing features. It was large—better than five feet, that much I knew. And it was not about to change course. Greatly concerned, I took a slow step back toward the skiff, and then another.

The shark moved toward me as inexorably as a boulder rolling downhill. Then there it was, a nurse shark, the Dumb Dora of the Keys' shark family. Too dumb to eat a fly but smart enough to once take a bite out of a mesh bag containing six freshly caught gray snapper that I had hung over the side of my skiff to keep them in perfect condition until dinner time. Feeling the skiff rock a bit, I'd looked over the side and seen the coffee-colored shark, its teeth gripping the bag, shaking its large head back and forth, trying to rip the bag apart with its rows of small, sharp teeth.

I had whacked that shark on the head with the billy club I kept aboard. Then again, even harder as it stared at me with its implacable shark eyes. Finally, reluctantly, it let go.

Now, as I backed toward Jeffrey's skiff, I wished for that billy club. I poked the shark's nose with the tip of my rod. No dice. The shark stayed right there, trying to decide what part of me to chomp. When, at long last, I reached the skiff, I hauled myself aboard with an agility I thought I'd lost long ago. The shark hung around for a while, then slid into the channel and vanished that eerie way they do.

I sat there on the deck, sprawled in the marvelous Keys' sunshine and waited for Jeffrey. He made it back in about an hour, leading a hooked bonefish that swam behind him like a dog on a leash. It was a fish, Jeffrey said, large enough to be weighed. Ten and a half pounds, a good bonefish for the lower Keys. Jeffrey was pleased.

That was a good thing for me. He didn't ask for details about my morning. On the way home, with the skiff up on a plane, zipping across thin water under that dazzling sun, I decided I'd cross bonefish off the list of fish I still wanted to meet. So far, the bonefish have cooperated with enthusiasm and consideration.

Tackle and Techniques

Although it's possible to catch many of the fish in this book while in pursuit of another, in no two cases are fishing techniques and fishing grounds more closely aligned than in the case of bonefish and permit. And perhaps no two species have captured the imagination of fly fishers as have these two fish of the tropical flats. An advertisement for fly rods seen in all the fly-fishing magazines these days shows an airport waiting line composed mostly of well-dressed businessmen. The last guy in line, however, wears fishing paraphernalia. Above the head of each man floats a cloud that tells his story. The message over the first head reads something like "He's got a big deal to close in Saudi Arabia." So it goes until we get to the last man—the only one who's smiling—whose face is lit up with a wild, fanatical grin. His caption reads "He's got an appointment with Mr. Bonefish at Something-or-other Cay, in the Caribbean."

It's easy to understand why people like these fish and this fishing. It's mid-November here in Maine as I'm writing this, and damned cold, but bonefish and permit couldn't be fresher in my mind. Yesterday, Capt. Steve Bellefleur and I were sitting at an open-air restaurant, built on the guide's dock in Islamorada. The temperature at breakfast time was 75 degrees, and the funky-looking older gent at the next table was tossing bits of his uneaten food to a pelican who looked as if he was accustomed to such treatment. The palm trees and mangroves along the shore, the glassy, warm-looking water, our scantily clad waitress—everything spoke of the Keys' tropical, laid-back lifestyle. As the last of the guides left with their clients to board a flats skiff and head off into the backcountry, Steve and I started north on U.S. Route 1 to the Miami Airport. The culture shock hit like a ton of bricks as we were waiting in Newark, New Jersey, for our flights up to New England. The waiting area in the express concourse was packed to overflowing with uncomfortable people separated only by the thickness of a briefcase or carry-on bag, each trying to hold onto a tiny bit of personal space. Express service travelers must first board a bus, which carries them out onto the airfield. They board in the style of the 1950s by walking up a ramp rolled to the rear of the plane. People were clearly relieved to head out into the cold, gray, New Jersey dusk just to get that much closer to home. Nothing against the North—I live there and I love it. What a pleasant change it is, though, when it's too cold to hold a fly line, and there's nothing left to hold it for anyway, to head south, down to Margaritaville, to fish the flats.

It's not just the weather that makes Keys' flats fishing for bonefish and permit so fabled; it's the fish themselves. Let's start with permit. I can think of no fish more revered by the fly-fishing community than this one; it possesses all the attributes of a truly remarkable game fish. First, permit grow to a great size. Fish of 40 or more pounds are not uncommon, and the average on the flats is probably close to 20 pounds. Second, it is by any account a tough customer—perhaps the toughest. Fly-fishing legend Joe Brooks caught some of the first on a fly 50 years ago. In his 1957 book *Greatest Fishing*, Brooks recounts stories of one of his contemporaries, an angler named Hagen Sands of Islamorada, tangling with four permit on the fly, probably around 1950. "The first, and largest, Sands estimated at 50 pounds and this baby hit and started for Europe and never did stop. He took everything Sands had in the line department, whisking it from the reel a mile a minute, the fly line, 200 yards of backing—then, zing! exit Mr. Permit. Three others around the 30 pound class, put up terrific fights, one of them taking Sands a mile out to sea before breaking off. Another got away in a hurry, and the fourth supplied the real heartbreak. Sands had his hand on the fish when it gave a last desperate wiggle and snapped the leader." Permit are elusive, wary beyond words, and more finicky about their food than a prize cat. Until recently, in fact, many anglers thought that permit took flies only by accident, not readily enough to be even worth fishing for. Modern techniques and exceptionally realistic fly patterns have changed that a bit.

The permit is a fish of southern waters. On the most unusual of occasions permit have been found as far north as Massachusetts, presumably riding on the Gulf Stream and sliding shoreward on a warm-water eddy. In general, though, permit are seldom found in any numbers north of Biscayne Bay. Guides all along the Keys feel that permit forsake the flats sometime in late spring to spawn. Some of the young, under an inch in size, become caught up in the Gulf Stream. *McClane's Standard Fishing Encyclopedia* reports that the smallest ones ever recorded were found in the Gulf Stream, one 360 miles off the coast of Virginia. Once the fish grow to a couple of inches they seem to move back inshore.

As adults, permit are not creatures of large schools, at least not while they're on the flats, and larger permit are often solitary creatures. To me they are among the most exotic looking of fish. No matter how they're held for photos, they always seem to have only two dimensions, just the length and height that create that enormous side-on profile. The dorsal and ventral fins, positioned directly over one another, sweep back at the same angle as the deeply forked tail, giving the fish the look of some kind of space vehicle rather than a common fish. The body of the permit is approximately half as tall as it is long, and it's extremely compressed side to side. It's so tall for a flats fish that it's not unusual to find the permit with a considerable portion of its back sticking out of the water. The narrow side-to-side profile makes a large permit look monstrous when removed from the water because the length and height dimensions must make up for its meager breadth. The permit is also a beautiful fish. Although color can vary, possibly changing depending on the bottom it's found on, they often have a deep blue back with silvery sides. The fins have a darkish appearance. The permit is a sight feeder without peer, and it has a very large and prominent eye located just in back of a blunt, thick-lipped mouth—perfect equipment for grubbing crabs from the bottom.

Often found side by side with the permit is the venerable bonefish. It's amazing to find that two fish with such similar habits and habitats could be so differently designed. Then again the southern flats contain a boundless array of species, including rays and sharks of all sizes and types. The bonefish are almost tubular in shape, have a deeply forked tail, chrome sides, greenish back with dark vertical bars, and one prominent flaglike dorsal fin. Like the permit, the bonefish has a prominent eye in back of and only slightly above a rubbery-lipped mouth, but the bonefish's mouth is far more underslung than a permit's. Both fish have powerful crusher plates in the back of their mouths for crushing the shells of crabs, shrimp, and lobsters. The snout of the bonefish is quite slender compared with the permit's, and the way the mouth runs back from it reminds one more than a little of a pig. Van Campen Heilner—whose favorite fish was the bonefish—said that a bonefish looked like a cross between a grayling and a carp; a chrome carp I would add.

Bonefish are purely neurotic. Although they are no more wary than a permit, bonefish never enjoy a calm moment. It's not unusual to see schools of bones moving across a large, shallow, turtle-grass flat with some individuals racing out in front of the school, their movements and messy rootings in the bottom frightening other members of the group. The whole nervous, undulating mass sends reverberating waves in all directions. The slightest disturbance—a passing bird or the plop of the minutest fly—can send the whole bonefish army into headlong retreat for deeper water.

It's quite a thrill to have the prick of your fly's hook be the instrument of their surprise. Bonefish, like bonito, will rocket around in figure 8s or reversing circles, alternately deeply bending the rod or causing you to believe that they're unhooked, before finally heading straightaway for the horizon on a 100- or 200-yard run that is guaranteed to test the best drag system. Nor are bonefish quickly subdued at boatside. Even without deep water to hang down in, bonefish are stubborn to the last.

Bonefish are not big fish compared with permit. But the Keys supply larger ones than do the Caribbean flats; no one raises an eyebrow at a 10-pounder, and they reach 13 or 14 pounds regularly. Bonefish of this ilk appear even bigger on the flats since their tubular bodies make a 14-pound fish upward of three feet long. Catching them, however, is far from a daily occurrence as these larger fish travel singly or in small groups and are as apprehensive as any creature on this planet.

The biology of the bonefish is uncommon. A larval bonefish has the long, thin shape of an eel, with its fins located back by its tail and its head connected by the ribbonlike body. Over a fairly short time the tiny bonefish shrinks to less than half its original length, its fins assume the position they will have in adulthood, and the miniature bonefish is formed. Because of their common occurrence in warm, shallow waters around the world, they are among the most important saltwater fly-rod game fish in existence. They are, however, fussy about their water, and are rarely found in areas outside their common range, or even far up into Florida Bay where an element of freshwater might occur.

Islamorada, located about a third of the way down the Florida Keys, is at the center of continental U.S. bonefishing activity. On the northwest side of the Keys lies Florida Bay. Down through central Florida a giant aquifer is created as the network of interconnected lakes and swamps drains constantly southward, finally becoming the river of grass, the Everglades, which exits into Florida Bay. The bay was land of sorts during the last ice age. What were once meadows and forests are now submerged grass-covered flats interspersed with mangrove hummocks and semisolid ground. The rich, brackish environment at the head of the bay is home to a variety of game fish, like redfish and snook, but seldom the bonefish, which prefer a more marine environment. The bay's nutrients, however, build a rich food chain that reaches down toward the beginnings of the Gulf of Mexico, where the bonefish and permit flats begin. At this point, rich expanses of dark turtle-grass flats stretch to the horizons. In the sunlight the dark flats appear purple, perhaps prompting the name Islamorada, which in Spanish means purple isle. The flats are intersected with cuts or channels that provide moving water and access to the deeper saltwater lakes that lie between the flats. Bonefish and permit move out of the sanctums of the lakes onto the flats, called by food, winds, currents, and water temperature intertwined in ways that are only partially understood by even the saltiest members of the famous Keys' guiding fraternity. There are literally miles and miles of productive bonefish and permit flats—some right up against the mainland areas of the Keys, some 15 miles out in the middle of Florida Bay, and many more here and there in between.

The Florida Bay–Gulf of Mexico side of the Keys is only half the picture. The Atlantic side has its particular and important features. Running about 6 to 10 miles off the east coast of the Florida Keys is the only living coral reef in the continental United States. Outside the 30-foot-deep reef the bottom plummets toward the deeper waters that house the Gulf Stream. Inside, however, exists a protected world. The bottom becomes gradually more shallow until within a mile or so of shore one encounters hard-bottomed coral reefs. These flats contain some soft areas and some regions of grasses, but generally this is hard coral bottom, festooned with weedy marine growth. The flats hold plenty of bonefish, including the bigger ones for which the Keys are famous. Some enormous schools of bonefish can be found here, and in cold weather it is believed that fish from both the ocean and the bay sides slide into the deep water between the flats and the reef looking for sanctuary. Because of the relatively firm nature of these flats, as well as a shoreline on the outside of the Keys that is more open than the mangrove-covered one on the bay side, shorebound anglers have better access and wading opportunities.

Picking the better spots on either the bay or ocean sides is a daunting task. Capt. Marc Bellefleur of Islamorada, our guide on a recent trip there, has spent the last 15 years poling every inch of the bonefish and permit flats in the upper and middle Keys. All of these flats, Marc told us, hold fish from time to time, but none of them do all the time. Every conceivable variable, luck of the draw included, comes into play when attempting to find the productive ones on any given day. One of the most important of the variables is water temperature. Bonefish and permit have narrow tolerance ranges for water temperature. In a land where water temperature is remarkably more stable than anywhere else along the U.S. mainland, the variance of a few degrees can be critical; this, according to Marc, is especially true if the water temperature drops much below 75 degrees. Cold winds from approaching high pressure can cool the shallow flats rapidly during the nighttime. During the day, however, the tropical sun quickly warms the dark-bottomed shallows. The oceanside flats are better buffered against cold because they have the heat reserves of the deeper, warmer waters near at hand. Some of this buffering effect is also gathered by moving farther down the bay side toward the Gulf of Mexico.

Because water temperature is so critical, the time of the year when you go fishing is also important. During some periods from November through March it is possible for the flats to be void of bonefish and permit. On the other hand, even during the dead of winter a few warm days can bring these predators back onto the flats. Catching such fish is more difficult; although they will scoff down baited hooks, they are reluctant to pursue an artificial. To some degree the farther down the Keys you go, the more protection you have from winter cold; it can, however, be a problem anywhere in the Keys. Oddly, though, few bonefish are found near the Key West end of the chain; the upper Keys, especially around Card Sound and Biscayne Bay—these bays are behind the Keys but north of Florida Bay—are renowned for their large bonefish. The best months are probably during spring and fall. The hot summer months bring windless dog days during which flats fish are less aggressive and hard to approach. The breezier conditions of fall and spring make casting more difficult, but it's easier to approach wary flats fish with the surface of the water broken by waves. You may not see them as easily, but they have the same problem seeing you.

With all this territory to consider, planning an approach is not easy. To decide which part, of which flat, at what tide, during which conditions, to fish for bonefish or permit requires a lot of knowledge. One rule is that these flats fish are less nervous, and therefore more likely to be tailing, during the hours of low light angle early or late in the day. Tailing occurs when a fish sticks its face down against the bottom to catch prey hiding there. The fish lifts its tail higher than its head—called tipping up—and the tail often sticks out of the water. Many species of fish can occasionally be found tailing, but it's far more common among flats fish. Tailing fish are visible, and they are intent on their feeding. Even though the low angle of light may make the fish tougher to see under the water, the tailing fish leaves little question about where it is or if it is interested in feeding.

When fish can't be seen tailing, they are often located by their mud—especially on deeper flats, like the ones between the oceanside flats and the reef. Muds are discolored areas of water made by the permit and bonefish rooting like hogs in the soft bottom. Often these areas are clearly visible, even from a fair distance.

But before we can see fish or muds we must select a flat, and then a part of the flat. Tides are important on both sides of the Keys but behave in different ways. The ocean side of the Keys experiences a rise and fall of two to three feet, twice daily. In the bay the complex web of bars and interlaced channels, the entrance of a great deal of freshwater from the Everglades, and the wind combine to make the timing of the tides and the depth of water far less predictable than on the ocean. Clearly, unless a flat holds enough water to float your boat, it means nothing to you. On the other hand, it helps if the water is shallow enough either to allow you to see the fish at a distance or to cause fish to be visible when they tip up on prey. Water clarity is also an issue. A heavy wind across either side of the Keys can dirty the water, especially nearshore where surf develops. This is even more of a problem on the soft flats of the bay.

Local experience is important in guessing what water conditions will be on the flats. The locals are also likely to know where the fish have most recently been. Bonefish and permit are habitual, sometimes for reasons that we understand and sometimes for ones that we don't. Bonefish establish repetitive daily habits that continue for an undetermined time. So it's far more likely that you'll be productive if you start by fishing flats where they were schooling yesterday, and the day before.

The size of a flat is also important as is its access to deeper water. Big flats, with good access to deep water, will hold big schools of fish. Big schools offer more targets, and because of the competition the fish are less wary and therefore easier to catch. If you look at a chart of Florida Bay you'll see places like Nine Mile Bank. This bank stretches around a large lake named Rabbit Key Basin. On the outside of the bank is the beginning of the open Gulf of

Mexico. This is an area of tremendous holding water as well as soft-bottomed feeding habitat, and it's not the only one like it in Florida Bay. It takes a complicated run through the backcountry to reach places like this, but once you're there the chances of running across bonefish, permit, or other game fish of the Florida flats are excellent.

Several other criteria are important in choosing a flat on which to begin fishing. Water temperature, wind, and tidal flow combinations are critical. For instance, let's say that this morning we have clear skies and a light wind from the north left over from a cold front that has blown itself out over the last few days. The tide is scheduled to be high at around noon; I say scheduled because in Florida Bay the wind, coupled with the complicated movements of the water inside the banks and channels, can make tide charts almost useless. The morning is likely to be tough, with cold water keeping the fish from tailing on the flats; we might want to be off the edges of the bank looking for muds in the warmer, deeper water. In the afternoon, though, the hot tropical sun of the Keys will raise the water temperature dramatically on the shallow, dark-bottomed flats. As the tide starts to drop from the bay, the game fish are likely to move up onto the downtide sides of the flats where they will meet the comfortable, warm water running off the flat.

As you select a direction to move along the flats you will also want to consider the probable direction of the game fish. The bonefish and permit will normally work either across or into the moving water, keeping them in clear water and away from the mud they are creating.

Now, based on all this information, Capt. Marc Bellefleur has selected a flat for us to fish. As he poles his skiff onto the flat, Marc becomes absorbed in putting all the pieces of this puzzle into an order that will show his clients bonefish and permit. The guide usually sees the fish before the angler. First, he's perched on his poling platform, several feet above the level of the angler on the bow. Second, he knows what he's looking at; he sees it every day. The flats are full of life—here comes a big ray, there's a bonnethead shark. These are good signs according to Marc—there's life on the flats. Sometimes bonefish and permit will move along in back of a ray to capture the crabs that the ray flushes from cover.

We come to a big hole in the flats; these holes may have been created by practice bombs dropped during the war or by erosion from an underwater spring. The holes are of different depths, and in some of them fish will rest or hide. Sometimes the fish in these holes feel comfortable because of the depth, and they'll allow you to approach closely. Marc thinks he sees a fish lying in the hole, and we cast to it; a small shark swims away from the fly and moves out of the hole onto the flat. On another occasion, however, a whole pod of bonefish turns up behind my fly, the biggest one darting out in front and taking the prize. During very windy days, or if it seems most productive that day, Marc may "stake out." Staking out involves sticking the long push pole into the bottom and tethering the boat to it with a cord at an advantageous casting angle to a sand hole or other area of high visibility. The anglers then wait for fish to move within casting distance.

Sometimes permit will station themselves in front of a cut, almost on the surface with their fins sticking out of the water. The fish survey the bottom for prey that may be moving through the cuts with the tide. In this scenario it is sometimes possible to take permit on flies presented well off the bottom. Usually a fly must be right on the bottom, but according to Marc, when permit exhibit this rare behavior they're much easier than normal to catch.

Many times bonefish are located by a "push" of water. The push is created when one bonefish, or more often a group, moves rapidly through shallow water. Schooling bonefish become competitive. Racing off in front of one another, they push a small wall of water in front of them as they hurry across the flats. Sometimes this behavior breaks out into tailing fish, and many are taken by first sighting the push. Often, though, the push comes from fish that have been frightened or are simply crossing the flat to reach some other spot. These fish will seldom stop for a fly and are nearly impossible to catch.

With either bonefish or permit, the most desirable circumstance is to find them tailing. Tailing fish are happy, feeding fish, often quite intent on the bottom in front of them. Under these conditions the fish are easier to approach and certainly more likely to take the fly. It doesn't always mean that they will, though. On the first day of our trip we had some good shots at both bonefish and a nice permit of about 20 pounds. These tailing fish were all over our #6 lead-eyed fur-strip worms but just wouldn't hit them. We stripped, we waited, we gave tiny jerks on the line, and nothing worked. The next couple of days we switched to small crab imitations, and we had more success. Perhaps with the falling temperatures that we were experiencing, the worms were digging in and the fish dialed in on crabs. Perhaps it was something else. Bonefish and permit have always been like that. A.J. McClane said, "One of the enigmas of the game is that bonefish will not respond to a bait for awhile; then on the next tide in the same place with the identical conditions of wind and sunlight they will hit nine casts out of ten."

Compared with most kinds of fishing, successful flats presentations require you to address more variables. It starts with the boat; even the noise of the smallest waves slapping against the hull of the boat can scare a bonefish or permit at the fringes of fly-casting range. In many cases the productive flats are covered by no more than two feet of water. The fish in such shallow water can see motions and hear sounds that fish in deeper water would not detect. Capt. Bellefleur told me, "Bring light blue shirts, it helps to be the same color as the sky." He went on to say, "You can talk quietly but don't allow anything to bump against the hull when we get close to the fish." If the fish are close, or if the sun is behind you, you should make the cast from a kneeling position, with the rod movements kept sidearm and low to the water. Under clear conditions the caster must make the presentation well out in front of the fish and let the fish swim up to the fly before starting the retrieve; if the cast lands too close to the fish it will scare it into the next state. Much has been written about flats-fishing legends who can cast into a teacup at 90 feet. I've yet to meet them; however, having good control out to 60 or 70 feet is helpful and worth practicing. It's also helpful to become competent at accurately making backhand casts; frequently circumstances will not allow a forehand shot. Again, practice makes perfect, and your lawn, not the bone-fish flats, is the place for practice. Tough though flats fishing may be, it's so rewarding when everything works out that I greatly enjoy the challenge.

Flies for permit and bonefish are made to simulate the wide variety of marine worms, crabs, shrimp of all sizes, and small fish—commonly called glass minnows in the South—that are found on the Keys' flats. Here are the fly designs that Marc likes for the flats around Islamorada. The worms, shown in figure 9.2, can be simulated by fur-strip flies about two inches in length tied on either size 2 or 4 hooks. Some should have lead eyes; some, for fishing on shallow flats, should not. All flies should have monofilament weed guards. Glass minnows are well imitated by small Clousers, and this fly will also work well as a small-shrimp imitation. Most crab patterns require a bit more effort to tie. I've made some that worked well by cutting out a small, dime-sized shell from a half thickness of a white scrubbing pad. Tie a short tail of fur strip on the underside of the hook down near the bend. Wrap the hook shank with thread, and attach lead eyes Clouser style. Wrap the shell material onto the opposite side of the hook from the lead eyes, so that the fly will ride shell up. Then thread some rubber legs between the fake shell and the hook shank and Pliobond them into place. You can dress up the shell by covering it with tan-colored sparkle fabric paint. Tie this fly on a size 4 hook for bonefish. Permit are bigger fish, and having some of these patterns tied on size 2 or 1 hooks is a good idea. Drab tan or olive is best; some flies should carry a bit of flash, but some should have none.

When you cast to bonefish, retrieve in short, little jerks that allow the fly to sink between movements; this seems to be the most effective. For permit cast a realistic crab pattern well in front of the fish. When the permit gets close give just enough short strips to get its attention, then stop; let the permit root your fly out of the bottom. This is the secret weapon that has made permit

Figure 9.2   *Marine worm fly.*

fishers so much more successful than they were when Joe Brooks stripped a white streamer in front of hundreds before he got a strike. If you head down to Islamorada, your guide or a local fly shop will have some of the area's favorites for you to try. I always bring my fly-tying vice on such trips so that I can whip up a few of the new hot flies.

The rod and reel requirements for bonefish and permit fishing in Islamorada are subject to a fair amount of variability. For strictly bonefishing, on a pleasant June day with light winds and excellent visibility, an 8-weight is perfect. Bonefish flies are quite small, but crab patterns are not aerodynamic. Although you might hook a 12-pound fish, there is no deep water to lift them up from, so you don't need a rod with a heavy butt. If it's blowing hard, though, an 8-weight is the minimum, and I like a 9 or 10. I caught a 10-pound bone on a 10-weight fly rod and didn't feel a bit like a bully. It's important for the fly to land delicately, especially on flat, calm days, and it helps for the line to have low visibility in the air. There may very well be an unseen fish between you and the one you're casting to; one panicked bonefish will make the whole school bolt for the exits.

Many guides like the clear intermediate lines. Any floating line, even a clear one, will create a line of disturbance on the surface of the water. That disturbance may only be a few inches above the head of a bonefish. The intermediate line will quickly sink—also important for fishing the sand holes—and become nearly undetectable in the water column. The line weight is actually more important than the rod weight. Because today's fast-action fly rods can handle a couple of weights of line ranging either up or down in size, you can handle the versatility requirements by having with you something like an 8-weight rod with an 8- and a 10-weight line.

Both bonefish and permit are reel smokers; that is, they can make long, fast runs against your reel's drag. Bonefish are usually good for one long run; 200 yards of backing should be plenty. Permit, on the other hand, can make a first run of 200 yards, pause, and then head off for another 100 or more. It is frequently necessary to chase permit with the boat to keep from being spooled. Using Spectra for backing material will allow you to add the extra backing necessary to handle these fish without going to a reel that is bigger and heavier than the rod weight warrants. Although I like an antireverse reel for most species that can make long, fast runs, light bonefish leaders require such a light drag setting that antireverse reels are left with no cranking power. The drag of an antireverse reel will usually slip more easily if the handle is being turned than if it isn't. Permit require a heavier leader and make an antireverse reel more practical because a heavier drag setting is called for.

Bonefish leaders should be about 10 feet long and have a 3-foot tippet that ends in no more than eight-pound test. You'll never live long enough to land a big permit on eight-pound test, especially in turtle grass, which will abrade your leader in no time. Twelve-pound test is more appropriate for permit.

An important piece of equipment is a stripping basket. One of the plastic baskets used by Northeast surf casters—the kind worn on a belt around the waist that we described in chapter 2—is helpful when standing on the bow of a flats boat on a windy day.

Once these fish take the fly it's best to set the hook with a "strip strike"— not lifting the rod but making a long steady pull until you know the fish is solidly on. Using this technique, if the fish misses the fly it's still there, and either it or another fish may still grab it. If you lift the rod in the air and the fish misses the fly, he's out of there—along with the rest of the school.

After the fish is on the line, though, you should hold the rod very high so the line will gather as little weed as possible and won't catch on mangrove stems that are growing on many of the productive Keys' flats. Bonefish and permit have mouths that are a fly fisher's dream—thick-lipped and rubbery— and flies readily sink in and hold very well. When either a bonefish or a permit takes the fly, you can be sure that it will make it to the reel. You may see some rapid changes of direction and have to make a few strips, but eventually these fish will head for the horizon. It's important once this happens not to squeeze the line too tightly; the lightest possible pressure is perfect. Once the fish takes off, hold your line hand well away from the reel and focus your attention on clearing the line lying around your feet. If you're stepping on it, or if it leaps up and snares the reel or rod butt, you're in trouble. Both fish have significant stamina at boatside and you're going to be using a fairly light tippet, so patience is the word. When the fish is ready a net is the best landing method for either fish. Some permit, however, are too big for most nets. Their large, forked tail makes them easy to tail, though.

Warm tropical waters hold less oxygen than cold, northern seas. It's important to revive these fish before releasing, especially if sharks are nearby. Gently hold the fish facing into the current. You'll feel it regain its strength and tug against your grip; the correct time for the release will be apparent. Be patient because it may take five minutes or longer.

Most people are familiar with the Florida Keys as a vacation area. These small islands support a vast amount of accommodations but can be very busy, especially from February through May, the prime tourist season. Airports are located at Key West, Marathon, and Miami; the latter is just under two hours' drive from Islamorada.

It is possible to fish this area from your own boat, but unless you have a very shallow draft boat and are competent with charts and reading the water, I wouldn't. The network of flats and channels is mind boggling, and to promote much needed ecological conservation many rules have been established to regulate boaters in the area. You are not permitted to run your outboard over some flats, even at idle. It's against the law to leave propeller trails on these flats because the grass may take many years to grow back. To avoid this you must follow small, unmarked channels that weave through the banks, and you must do this by reading the water. On top of these difficulties you must then find fish. Unless you're planning an extensive trip, and therefore have plenty of time on your hands, I'd hire a local guide. It's a big industry in the Keys. Many local guides are available, but they book up in advance, so call ahead.

Other than the tackle that we've mentioned, most special equipment for Keys' flats fishing consists of things to help you survive the tropical sun. Many of the guides who live with this sun every day wear surgical masks to cover their faces; many of the older guides have passed away from cancers that started on their skin. I wear sun gloves—a fly-fishing glove that leaves your finger tips exposed—long-sleeved shirt, flats-style hat with ear-covering flaps, and polarized glasses with side shields, and I cover every exposed inch of me with a heavy-duty sunscreen. I also bring a foul-weather suit that I wear on the way out on cool mornings or if it rains.

Many anglers have taken these game fish in the Keys while wading. I've not done it, and the locals don't recommend it. First, the bay flats are simply too soft for wading without snowshoes or the like. Second, the firmer ocean flats have limited access, although some good flats run right out from the oceanfront hotels at which you might be staying. Nonetheless, you can wade, and there are some areas of public access. Starting at zero in Key West, the road through the Keys is set off by mile markers. Long Key State Park is near mile marker 60 and has two miles of wadable shoreline. Bahia Honda State Park has access to wadable flats from around mile marker 40, and a stretch called Long Sands provides flats access right off the highway for a considerable stretch along Lower Matecumbe Key. Waders in the Keys should shuffle their feet—not step up and down—move slowly, and wear flats booties. The flats have stingrays and sea urchins, the sting of which can not only hurt but also partially paralyze waders. One tip for waders by Marc Bellefleur is to find a flat where fish are moving along and then wait. The fish move so much on the flats that Marc feels you will catch more by quietly waiting for the fish to come to you; this will certainly give you good shots at happy fish when they come by.

Chapter
10

Tarpon—
Key West,
Florida

*T*he one place in the Florida Keys where you can almost always count on being able to see wild tarpon swimming free is just a few steps from the Overseas Highway—that rather grand name for the narrow ribbon of arching bridges and two-lane road that connects more than 100 miles of islands, mangrove hammocks, and uncounted square miles of splendid fly-fishing waters. Driving "down" the Keys from Largo to Key West after you leave Islamorada and cross the Lignum Vitae Bridge, watch for the turnoff to your right at mile marker 77.5; it's the first turnoff you can make in Lower Matecumbe.

There should be a sign there (there always has been) that says "Fresh Fish" and another that tells you that boats are for rent. But no sign tells you about the tarpon. As marinas go in south Florida and the Keys, the place is a modest, no-frills enterprise with a direct approach to its daily business: buying, selling, and shipping fresh fish; serving fish and chips to hungry travelers; and renting well-seasoned small craft to anglers, divers, and other adventurers who happen by. The wooden dock is narrow, and its well-weathered planking tilts a bit.

At the dock's end where a gas pump waits to fuel the rental fleet, tarpons gather. If you sit at the edge of that dock's sun-silvered planking at high tide, your feet will swing just a few inches above 15 or 20, or perhaps even 30, great silver fish turning lazily in the clear waters, gliding into the shadows beneath the dock, then reappearing, catching sunlight on their incandescent scales.

They make a stunning assembly, these creatures that speak of prehistory even as they communicate elemental grace, fluid within fluid, somnolent yet charged. Some are giants, close to seven feet, awash in their awesome girth. Others pivot more swiftly, profligates spending youth's energy. Like migrant souls of the sea, the tarpon appear and disappear without haste, sliding back and forth through their veil of waters in this most unlikely spot to witness a silver enchantment.

One of the most impressive giants among them has a disfigured cheek: not a shocking scar, but enough of an anomaly to catch the eye of a careful observer when the fish rolls on its side. The several intricate bony lines that define the etched and embossed exterior anatomy of the tarpon's chitinous gill plates have been wrenched from their original symmetry. A section of the plate flares in permanent disharmony, torn from its moorings in an earlier mishap and unattended since.

It is a scar of capture. The giant took an angler's lure years ago, was boated and released with a wrench that tore the hook from its mouth and gills. Perhaps traumatized, the great tarpon took refuge beneath the dock. People tossed it fish heads, guts, racks, and tails—by-products of the fish market. As months passed and the free food kept coming, the fully recovered resident fish was joined by more of its brethren. What communication prompted these gatherings is a mystery; the small cove is not typical of tarpon water. Nor are these sedentary creatures; they are more wild bird than fish in their migratory restlessness, flowing in vast silver rivers through the dark oceans of the southern seas on long voyages triggered by that most ancient of compulsions—the reproduction of the species.

Nevertheless, here is proof that 20 or 30 or more tarpon have stepped out of the ranks of their wild schools and made a home within earshot of the Overseas Highway. Like the fish themselves, first one and then more human visitors traveled to this small dock to watch the daily feeding and toss tidbits into the gleaming tarpon turmoil.

What began as circumstance has become more formalized. Buckets of precut fish are available (for a fee) to visitors who would feed these tarpon. Like a sorcerer's wand, a bit of sliced yellowtail tossed off the dock's end transforms the assembled giants. Galvanizing what had been a circling ballet set to slow music of the spheres, the tidbit generates ferocity where there had been indolence, and a quickness too fast to follow. Instead of apparent domesticity, there is unmistakable wildness, a feral response so rapid and so merciless that watching it seems almost an invasion of the tarpon's privacy.

For anglers who have tried to entice wild tarpon to take a fly, there is much to be learned here. Do the fish turn on their side to strike, or do they merely open their great, undershot jaws and inhale? Is their feeding a heedless frenzy of compulsive strikes, the sort of instinctive behavior that prompts a 200-pound creature to swallow a few feathers on a small hook?

After hours of watching, it is still difficult to answer these questions. Yes, a few fish do roll on their sides, the sea green of their broad backs becoming the great sheet of gleaming silver that is their deep side, a torso so broad and so bright that in the clarity of shoal water it catches and holds the entire heavens above, reflecting the midday sun in a field of cerulean blue. This may be what prompts a guide to shout, "There! One flashed!" when a tarpon turns on its side in the wild. "It flashed on your fly! Did you see that?"

But here beneath your hanging feet at the end of this narrow dock, another six-foot tarpon swallows a morsel with little more than a nearly imperceptible opening and closing of that oddly shaped mouth, that unmistakable tarpon mouth with the protruding lower jaw that all but encloses its upper counterpart. This tarpon does not roll but maintains its perfect verticality. The jaws open and shut so quickly you have to ask yourself if you saw them. But the morsel has vanished.

Is this how tarpon take a fly? There are, you learn, no certainties. Sometimes they will roll. Other times they will come straight ahead and gulp. Then here is a tarpon nudging its morsel through the water, its protruding lips shut tight, pushing first this way, then that, the way an infant in a high chair might toy with its toast. Is this how a tarpon reacts to a fly? If so, anglers can find little cause for high hope.

Spend a half hour at the end of this dock, the sun high overhead, the water's surface unblemished by any breeze, and the tarpon below you could be specimens under glass. Each feature is detailed—paired nostrils, jet hemispheres of eyes as dark as night set in silver. Marvel at the tarpon's dorsal, that wavering lily stalk, its last ray a long, swept-back filament waving above the exotic hint of violet in the scales that arch across this creature's broad back. Note the sweeping scythe of a tail, its extended width greater than the span of the tarpon's breadth from back to belly.

These are an ancient clan, among the oldest of all swimming species, come to our millennium from 10 millennia beyond, arrived essentially unchanged from prehistory. The tarpon have outlived time and carry themselves with the dignity that such vast age bestows.

As I watch, realizing there are no certainties for the fly fisher, a visitor quartet walks down the dock from the shed where fish and chips are sold. They have been told of the tarpon and arrive with their buckets.

"Oh, my God!" shouts the rail-slim woman in her Bernardo sandals and Ralph Lauren resort shorts as she deciphers the great dark shapes wavering beneath the surface. "Come here, Andre. You've never seen anything like this. There. See them. Can you get them?"

"I'll try," says the tanned man with dark hair, raising a video camcorder to his shoulder, peering into the eyepiece capped with sponge rubber. "I've never tried shooting fish underwater."

A tarpon rolls, its bulk rocking like a massive cradle on the surface, its huge scales each clearly defined. "You can get that one," the woman exclaims, "He's half out of the water." Her arms tighten around her tiny waist, her hands reaching for each other around her rib cage as if they could meet at her spine. She is thrilled at the elemental grandeur she has discovered in this unlikely place.

"What kind of fish are these?" she calls out to the young man who acts as dockmaster.

"Tarpon," he answers. "They're tarpon." He is surprised anyone needs to ask.

"Can you catch one for me?" the woman asks. "Can you hook one from here?"

The question throws him. "Why?" he asks.

"They are so beautiful, so lovely," she says, still hugging herself and leaning over the edge of the dock. "I want to take one home with me. It could be like a painting on our wall."

He shakes his head slowly, thinking everything he has heard about tourists must be true. "No, you cannot kill these fish. They are protected. You must have a permit. But," he looks at the woman, "I'm not killing any of these fish here."

Soon the quartet returns to their car with its New York plates, the lovely, thin young woman still chattering as they go.

I understand her wonder, for there is no fish more spectacular, more awesome than the tarpon seen at close quarters in the clear, shoal waters off the Keys.

I am reminded of a calm Key West morning a half hour before sunrise when Capt. Michael Pollack steered his Maverick past the breakwater at the harbor entrance. It takes less than five minutes for a fast boat to reach the Northwest Channel off Fleming Key. As they do on many of Key West's placid May mornings on the flood tide, great silver tarpon roll here between the buoys, which is what they were doing as we approached. Michael shut down the outboard, and we drifted silently on the tide.

"We can both cast," he said, slipping an anchor silently over the stern and paying out line until we fetched up within 30 feet of a surfacing tarpon with silver shoulders as wide as a Rolls-Royce fender.

I get the shakes. It's what happens when I'm that close to large tarpon. I began waving my rod like a flagman trying to stop an out-of-control locomotive. "Easy, man. Easy," Michael says.

"Slow down. There are fish all around us."

I manage a 40-foot cast. Wham! A tarpon eats the James Brown almost before my first strip. I yank back, attempting a strike.

Bango! Fly line hisses from its heap on the deck. Miracle! I have the fish on the reel and watch, numb, as backing vanishes.

"Way to go," Mike yells from the bow. Then he shouts, "Whoa! Double-header." Michael strikes his fish the way it should be done, three mighty yanks, low, straight, and powerful, the line tight in his left hand. That hook is set, for sure.

But not mine. My tarpon jumps about a half mile off. His tail clears the windless surface, his great lightning bolt of a torso suspended there, bright against the still dusky western horizon. It tumbles back to the sea, white foam rising at the spot. Then he is gone. My line lies limp in the water, the rod lifeless in my hands.

Michael laughs. "Hey John, you forgot to bow. You should have bowed when he jumped. You know that." He pumps his rod, bent almost double as he leans into his fish. He begins the first word of still more lecturing when something quite wonderful happens. The tip section of his brand new Sage slips free. Tips have done that to me. Their joining with the butt section loosens, you forget to check, and eventually the rod simply separates, most of the time when it's under stress.

What you have to do then is fight the fish on the butt section, watching as the tip slides down the line, hoping to retrieve it when, at last, you land the fish and the tip has slid all the way to the leader, stopped there by the tarpon's nose.

Michael's contortions as he battles his tarpon with half a rod are most satisfying.

"This is a brand new Sage. Uunnnnh! Got to get that tip back. Uunnnnh! This is their best rod. Uunnnh!"

About 150 feet off our starboard side, a green can buoy marks the channel's eastern edge. It is about to become a player in our little drama. Doubling back on its long run north, Mike's tarpon heads south, fast, and wide to the east, out on the buoy's far side.

"No! Please, no!" shouts Michael as he feels the vibrations of his line grating on the buoy's anchor chain. "Please, God, no!"

Divine intervention is not forthcoming. As the leader scrapes past the rusted, barnacled chain, the monofilament parts without so much as a quiver. Michael's new rod tip drifts easily down the now fishless line, tilts off the end of the broken leader, and begins its final, silent voyage to the 20-foot-deep channel's murky bottom.

For at least two long, poignant minutes, Michael stares mutely at the butt section he still holds in his hands. Then he slumps and steps down from the bow.

There are so many things I could have said. Instead, I opt for silence. After all, our day has just begun.

I've put in a great many days fishing for tarpon. That one has to rank right up there near the top, and I remember every one. That's the thing about these fish. Their sheer size, the majesty of their procession across a flat, the slow dance of their rolling, that flash of silver, the sibilance of their breathing, and the incredibly sudden speed of their departure when alarmed combine to create an unforgettable portrait of a creature quintessentially wild.

How lucky we are they will eat a fly. They're well worth a rod tip every now and then.

Tackle and Techniques

Although a 40-pound permit or striped bass is a big fly-rod fish, the only actual big-game fish in this book is the tarpon. Tarpon grow to immense size, some over 200 pounds, and some are taken on fly rods every year that go well over 150. Tarpon can do it all: they can jump—10 feet vertically and 20 feet horizontally, according to McClane—they can run for distance, and they offer the most stubborn resistance of almost any fish that can be taken on a fly rod. Once hooked, many anglers have seen a huge poon simply blow off 300 yards of 30-pound backing before coming to the end and breaking off, all this before the guide could pull his push pole from the mud and give chase. Other tarpon orbit the boat, jumping continually until they finally land on the leader and achieve freedom that way. In rare cases—though it has happened—a six-foot, chrome-plated tarpon has landed wildly thrashing inside the angler's boat. The anglers then either run for the poling platform or jump out of the boat altogether, because a big tarpon's tail can break legs even more easily than it can rip out chairs that have been bolted to the deck, although it can do either. Stories abound of anglers requiring an hour and a half to land a 125-pound fish, though the pros can often do it in one minute for every 10 pounds of the fish's body weight. Tarpon subjected to long fights may be difficult to revive, and the ever-present sharks easily catch them.

Despite their great size and fighting capability, tarpon readily strike on comparatively small flies. Tarpon are often caught by live-bait anglers using some good-sized mullet. Blind casting the large flies that we use for stripers into the right kinds of places will produce, but this isn't the type of fly fishing that's done for tarpon in Key West. Here, tarpon emerge from deep water to swim along the warm, shallow edges of the flats, and anglers can add to their pleasure the thrill of sight casting to truly mammoth fish. I've seen them in the morning performing a routine called daisy chaining, whereby big tarpon swim in a circle, practically nose to tail, periodically making troutlike, head-and-tail rises that reveal black eyes the size of tennis balls. This display is thought to be a sort of courtship dance, fish style. When the tarpon are engrossed in daisy chaining you can get close, close enough to unnerve many an otherwise experienced fly fisher. The guides will tell you that many excellent casters become useless shadows of their actual selves at the sight of several dozen mammoth tarpon porpoising just off the bow of a flats boat.

Tarpon are strange fish. Apparently they are of ancient design, untouched by the evolution that has molded many other fish. They are from the herring family, and look like an enormous herring or shad. The body of the tarpon is covered with heavy scales of large diameter that give the fish an almost armored appearance. Like the herring they have only a single dorsal fin, but its last ray extends out into a long, thin strand that reaches almost to the tail. Tarpon even have an air bladder that they can fill while rolling on the surface; in tarpon talk this is called gulping air. You can sometimes hear tarpon gulping as they roll on a calm flat. This adaptive feature allows the tarpon to live in the stalest water, like the numerous roadside canals of southern Florida. Keeping a big tarpon from gulping air during the last stages of playing it allows the angler to subdue the fish more quickly. Sometimes tarpon are located by the release of air bubbles from this bladder as they swim underwater.

Tarpon are found on both warm-water sides of the Atlantic, rarely north of Virginia, although they are common off the Virginia Eastern Shore during the warmest part of summer. Despite what appears to be a shallow-water courtship, tarpon are thought to spawn offshore. The young, eel-like larvae of the tarpon are so unlike the adult form that they were at one time attributed to an entirely separate genus than the adult tarpon. Tarpon grow slowly; one fish caught in the Florida Keys during the 1930s is reported to be alive in an aquarium more than 60 years after it was captured. Because tarpon live so long and take nearly 10 years to reach reproductive age, the species would be susceptible to fishing pressure were it not that its flesh is considered unpalatable, at least here in the United States.

The area around Key West possesses some of the finest tarpon water in the world. Unlike the dark waters of the Central American rivers, the comparatively deep flats of the Florida west coast, or the muddy backwaters of the Everglades, the Keys provide expansive, warm, shallow flats that offer excellent habitat for the tarpon while at the same time providing the angler with helpful visibility. These flats are interlaced with cuts and channels that provide the large predators acceptable cover and resting places, and the grassy-bottomed, nutrient-laden environment feeds the tarpon well on its spring and summer northward migrations.

Another part of what makes the Key West area such fertile tarpon ground is that it represents both the southern and western tips of the continental United States landmass. Tarpon emerging from the Gulf of Mexico or the Caribbean may find these flats before all others, and then follow them up the

Keys before dividing onto the two coasts of mainland Florida. This is a migration that starts in late March and ends sometime in July. Along the way veteran guides have discovered numerous areas where the tarpon may be intercepted.

Tarpon are primarily nocturnal feeders. All through the Keys' many interconnecting channels tarpon may be found feeding in the middle of the night, especially in places where baitfish or shrimp are attracted to light sources and corralled for easy plunder between bridge pilings or in shadow lines. This feeding activity does not necessarily come to a halt on the morning flats, and it's not unusual to see tarpon chasing baitfish to the surface. As the tarpon swim over the flats during the day, they invariably run across small baitfish and crabs or shrimp that are living in the turtle-grass flats. The tarpon will feed opportunistically on this forage, and it is the imitation of these baits that is the most likely application of fly fishing the flats. Note that the lower jaw of the tarpon extends beyond the upper—a superior mouth, compared to the underslung, inferior mouth of a bonefish—and therefore tarpon are far less likely to head lower in the water column for a fly. They simply aren't built for scrounging the bottom; in fact, tarpon are often surface feeders.

During certain stages of the moon, the tarpon can also be found bingeing on paolo worms. Worm hatches—actually the spawning movements—of marine worms are important to many fisheries up and down the coast. That fish of over 100 pounds will sip these spindly, three-inch worms is amazing, but they sure do. The worm hatch can simply turn the fish on and make normally hesitant or finicky fish voracious. The better guides can anticipate the general time of these hatches and show their lucky clients some exciting tarpon fishing.

To describe exactly where and when to fish for tarpon in the Key West area is a tall order. First, I believe that to fish successfully on the flats of the lower Keys for tarpon, or most flats fish, you must have a guide—at least for a few trips. A vast amount of terrain is involved. Before trailering a boat to Key West and trying it on your own, you should get an idea of what you're in for. But a couple of areas seem to have tarpon consistently, and are not too complicated to get to or to fish with a fly rod.

The Marquesas Keys, 20 or so miles west of Key West, are perhaps the most exciting tarpon water in all the Keys. The Marquesas is a large, circle-shaped area of mangrove islands surrounding a shallow area of grass flats and an anchorage called Mooney Harbor. Several moderately deep channels pass through all but the north side of the Marquesas. Currents flow quite rapidly through the cuts and channels. Combined with the expansive flats of ideal depth, they create a complete habitat for migrating tarpon. In truth, on many late spring and early summer mornings all that is required for some excellent tarpon fishing is to be on the flats, near the channel outflows, with your eyes open, since tarpon often roll on the surface during early morning hours.

Once in the Marquesas an angler can also stake out near a strategically located patch of white sandy bottom—the tarpon will be clearly visible against the sand—and wait for the tarpon to pass by. Points where tarpon moving along an edge may be forced around a shallow area and passageways between deeper bodies of water can be good locations to wait for the tarpon to make perfect casting targets of themselves. It's important to choose locations that will give you the best possible visibility without similarly advantaging the fish; make sure that your shadow will not be projected onto the fish, and that you aren't so close to the fish that they will see you casting. Being quiet is also important if you want to cast to unsuspicious, happy fish.

Reaching the Marquesas is a bit easier said than done. The dawn trip from Key West passes through the winding channel of the Lake's Passage; it can be almost impossible for a pilgrim. And the ocean trip around the Atlantic side of the Keys can be treacherously rough in a flats boat. One day John, our guide, and I sped across the 30-foot-deep Boca Grande Channel that runs between the Marquesas and Boca Grande Key. When we had safely crossed to the other side of channel John was wearing a sort of nervous smile.

"John," I said, "what are you smiling at?"

"Oh," said John, "I was just thinking about all of those big hammerhead sharks that we just passed over." It's not every day that you can make this passage, and there are many days when you shouldn't try. Experience with the local weather patterns, and what they mean to boaters, is something else you get with the guide's fee.

The Marquesas Keys are not the only fishable waters west of Key West. Not by a long shot! A large area on the ocean side of Woman and Man Keys, just east of Boca Grande Channel, is pure sand bottom. Although tarpon passing over these flats are often fussy and nervous, it can be a great place to see as well as catch tarpon. Numerous other locations are within a short flats-boat ride of Key West.

Tarpon, unlike bonefish, will not be engaged in something so obvious as tailing along a shallow flat. Nonetheless, their activities in shallow water can make them quite visible. First, you may see them simply rolling and gulping air. Second, nervous water—ruffled areas on the surface caused by the underwater movements of these large fish—coupled with the occasional showing of the tip of a tail or the dorsal fin may give the fish away. Tarpon may sometimes "lay up" in dark, shallow water. When laid up—floating motionless on the surface—they will often lie with their tails and dorsal fins visible. I remember seeing a group of tarpon laid up on the north edge of Mooney Pond, right in the middle of the Marquesas. Some fish floated with one fin above the water, others with two, and still others were mere shadows, lying like logs just below the water's surface. Finally, tarpon are frequently located simply by poling a flat that is deep enough to hold such large fish and has sufficient visibility for the angler to see the fish occasionally before they see the boat. This is tough stuff, because large fish like tarpon are spooky as the devil in shallow water, but it can be done. Though I've seldom been successful with this approach, it's one that has accounted for many tarpon over the years. Unlike bonefish or permit, tarpon often frequent water so deep that little or nothing shows on the water's surface to give them away, even though they're on the move.

Tarpon on the flats can be spooky and hard to present to. As with all flats-inhabiting fish, it's best to keep the fly line from landing over the fish or from flashing in the air over the fish's head. The presentation must be innocuous. Here are a few things that you can do to keep from scaring the tarpon that you cast to. Make sure of your target and its direction, and don't cast until you know where you want the fly to land. Tarpon are known to like a fly that scurries away just in front of them, as a small fish or crab that they'd scared off the bottom might do. They are not likely to turn back and take a fly that had been presented behind them. Be aware of the effect that your fly may have on other fish. If you line one fish while casting to another, the whole school may bolt; this may also happen if your poorly made cast to the lead fish ends up being retrieved right at another fish in the school. Although it's hard to believe that a 1/0 fly could scare a 100-pound fish, believe it, especially if the fly is heading right for a tarpon in shallow water. If you make a cast that might cause this to happen, you'd often be better off to let the line sink and allow the fish to pass over and by it before retrieving. If you're staked up over sand, you'll often see the fish coming well in advance. Perhaps the most realistic presentation possible is to cast well in advance of the fish—especially if there are no weeds on the bottom to foul your fly—and start your retrieve just as the fish get close to the fly. This is as perfect a simulation of the behavior of a flushed baitfish as it's possible to provide. Although we'll be talking about flies in a minute, the use of a seemingly tiny fly is often best on the flats. Tarpon, especially happy, slow-swimming tarpon in shallow water, just don't react well to having a big fly dumped into their midst. Whatever you do, as one of my guides once advised, the farther away from the boat that you make the presentation, the better off you'll be. The reflection of the boat or the slap of a wave against a hull may unnerve the fish. They may not bolt, but they won't be happy either and will refuse to strike. If the fish were 80 feet from the boat rather than 30, you'd be much less likely to be detected.

Keys' style tarpon flies have been almost an art form unto themselves. I don't really know how far back the current designs and color schemes go, but it's quite a ways. I find the general lack of realism in tarpon flies reminiscent of Atlantic salmon concepts because the patterns of the flies often make little sense when compared with the fish's natural food. A salmon angler might say that he "rose him on a Jock Scott," but what could this colorful arrangement of hair and feathers possibly look like to the salmon? What living thing in or out of the river looks anything like a Jock Scott, or Blue Charm, or Green Highlander? Yet salmon strike them, probably mistaking them for some edible morsel—though the ancient debate rages about whether it's feeding, remembrances of feeding, or just plain bad temper that causes a spawning-run salmon to take any fly. A similar observation could be made about tarpon flies like the Black Death, Gotcha, or Ghunka. (The Black Death fly is shown in figure 10.1.) There's little doubt here that the tarpon sees these flies as food of some kind, and on the flats they see them clearly. In my view it's simply further evidence of how consistently we anglers overestimate the brains of our beloved fish, and how we mistake well-honed survival instincts for intellect. Often, if a fly moves seductively, is easily catchable, and is eating size, then the fish simply eats it, whatever it is.

Figure 10.1 *Black Death fly.*

A new generation of Keys' tarpon guides, however, is applying the more sophisticated bonefish and permit patterns to tarpon flies. Crabs are becoming more common, and I'd guess that pulling some realistic crab pattern from the sand in front of an oncoming tarpon would have better odds than making the same moves with some garish combination of purple and orange feathers. A movement toward refinements like eyes, realistic color patterns, and seductive materials like fur strips seems to be occurring. Some guides have told me that these new flies will, at times, succeed in drawing strikes when older patterns fail.

In any case, it's vital when tarpon fishing to use a hook that is both strong and very sharp. Carefully sharpening the hook on the outside of the point will make it stick better, and flattening the barb will help it penetrate. Many have compared setting the hook into the mouth of a tarpon to penetrating a cinder block. My early tarpon-fishing experiences returned to me many hooks so badly bent out—this happens when you pull hard on a hook that has penetrated only to the tip of the point—that I threw them out. If I had tried to salvage the fly by bending the hook back into shape, it would be even weaker next time. Hooks made of stout wire, and with a deep pocket, are available. These hold better and provide a better hooking angle than some of the hooks that are commonly used (see figure 10.2). After I started tying tarpon flies on these stout hooks, my landing ratio improved dramatically.

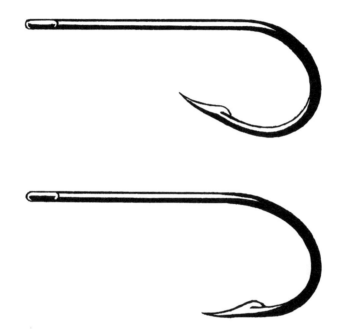

Figure 10.2 *Bends like the one on top hook more fish because the pull to the point is in a more direct line; they hold better, too, because of the deep, almost circular pocket.*

Even a sharp hook must be set hard into the mouth of a tarpon. Anglers, including some famous ones, are often seen making repeated sweeping hook sets to drive the point home. To a large degree they are simply bending their rods. You should instead point the rod almost directly at the fish and set the hook by pulling hard with the line hand. If you find that you are able to bring the rod back much over 30 degrees from the direction of the line, then you'd be better off stripping in a few more feet of line before making another sweep. Obviously, you must be wary of snapping the tippet should the fish start its run, but unless you have the line wrapped around your hand, it's difficult to break a fresh, well-tied 20-pound-class tippet. This is good advice for any fishing done with an indelicate tippet.

The tackle of tarpon fishing is essentially the heaviest-weight equipment that you can routinely cast, and that's even understating it a bit. Only the short, thick-butted, big-game rods used for sailfish and marlin are more powerful. Tarpon fishing is not like fishing for striped bass, when you might need a 12-weight rod to throw a 600-grain head, so that you could fish a big fly near the bottom in 20 feet of water. In tarpon fishing you need the big rod not to cast the fly but to handle the fish. Much has been said about using rods like three-piece 10-weights for tarpon, but the butt sections are simply too light, especially if you use 20-pound-test tippets.

Good fly-fishing guides have tackle for their clients to use. I suggest that unless you start doing a lot of it, or are going to go from your own boat, you let the guide provide the tackle. If you decide to get your own, let me suggest that tarpon tackle is not the gear to stock with unknown or budget products. You want a famous-maker rod, designed for tarpon fishing, and a reel that holds at least 300 yards of 30-pound-plus backing. As I mentioned earlier in the book, if the reel will hold that much 30-pound Dacron, then it will hold at least that much 50-pound-test Spectra, and that's what I'd use, especially with a 20-pound-test tippet. Dacron is comparatively fragile stuff, and it wouldn't take much to weaken 30-pound Dacron to the point where it would break before a fresh 20-pound mono tippet. This would cause you to lose the whole fly line, not to mention possibly dooming the tarpon. I personally prefer an antireverse reel for tarpon fishing. These fish are powerful and quick, and you could bust a knuckle or pop a tippet, or both, on a direct-drive reel. Early in my collecting of heavy-duty rods I bought the kind with foregrips. They're unnecessary in my view, and I rarely use them anymore. Many experts feel that they hamper to some degree the rod's casting ability.

Unless you're used to casting a 12-weight, you should get out and practice with it before your tarpon trip. The reciprocating weight of such an outfit is not burdensome for a good caster, but the torque developed by loading the rod is surprising. The line can easily slip through your fingers as your casting stroke changes direction; this unloads the rod and will ruin the cast. For another thing, the line fairly leaps through the guides, unlike its action in a lighter outfit in which you must work out the line over a number of false casts. This is actually a benefit, but you must be familiar with it or your line control will suffer. The answer is to practice, on the lawn if that's what's available.

Tarpon leaders are special pieces of equipment. Because of their rough mouth, a tarpon can quickly abrade even an 80-pound-test shock tippet. Here is one of the best applications for fluorocarbon material that I've seen. I must admit that I've not tried fluorocarbon as a chafing material on tarpon, but I've heard many reports from credible sources who say it's the answer. Some say that you can drop all the way to 40- or 50-pound test and lose very few tarpon. My approach would be to try both heavy and light tippets, using the heavier ones first until I had a refusal. Because tarpon leaders require complicated knots, are kept on a stretcher to keep the heavy shock tippets straight, and frequently have the shock leader snelled to the hook, they are typically tied up in advance.

These leaders are a lot of work to tie up, and with fluorocarbon they're not cheap. The tarpon leader is attached to the butt leader with a three-foot extension of 30-pound-test mono. After only one fish the bite tippet may be chafed beyond usability. Some may think me excessively frugal, but I've caught fish by simply clipping off the damaged portion of the bite tippet and tying on another piece of heavy material with a double surgeon's knot. You'll not be able to keep such a tippet within the IGFA rule of 12 inches, including the knot; however, it allows you to get back into action quickly. You can buy the pieces of prestraightened shock material by the clump. You can also make your own by dipping the material into boiling water and then hanging a length with a weight attached, later cutting it into the desired lengths. The slightest nick or fray in the class tippet or the butt extension requires an immediate change of leader.

It's possible to land most tarpon more quickly than people would imagine. When I first tried some of the aggressive fighting techniques that I'm about to discuss—these were not invented by me—I landed two tarpon of about 90 pounds each in 20 minutes, including time for casting and hooking up. Here are the elements you should use to achieve these results. First, you must make your mind up to pressure your leader fully. A 20-pound-test tippet is tougher than you imagine, unless it's cut or jerked without the cushioning effect of the rod. A tarpon guide once told me that you can't break 20 if there is any bend at all in the rod. I've not tried to break 20 while placing a bend in the rod; I started to once but chickened out. The pressure was so great that I was sure the rod was ready to explode, and the part of the rod forward of the second stripper guide followed the line as straight as an arrow. Despite the pressure that I'd applied, I'm confident that the 20-pound-test line was well below its breaking point. So if you keep a bend in the rod you are almost guaranteed not to break off your fish. That said, if you put much of a bend in the rod you'll never put on the pressure you need to subdue the fish quickly. To win these battles quickly, you must come as close to straight lining the fish as you dare; you must use only the very butt of your rod. The earlier in the fight that you exact that kind of pressure, the shorter the fight will be. Although I've not done this, I know that some tarpon anglers even pull the fish over backward in the air. They claim it breaks the fish's spirit. Again, the secret is not to do it without the shock-absorbing power of the rod, and you must use 20-pound test.

The angler must consistently pull on the fish opposite the direction the fish wants to go: lift a fish that dives, go "down and dirty" on a fish near the surface, and pull left or right in opposition to the fish's intended direction.

These tactics prevent the fish from rising to the surface for a gulp of extra oxygen, and disorient as well as discourage it. It may seem less sporting to some, but I disagree. The result is to reduce the length of the fight and allow the angler to release a fish that will recover more quickly than one that has been worn down over a longer time. I don't believe that such tactics are unsporting, especially because the angler is using only a fly rod on such a huge fish. Some anglers, to avoid the ordeal of the struggle for both themselves and the tarpon, will enjoy the first jump or two of the fish, then point the rod directly at it and yank back to break the tippet. If the fish is hooked in the lip it will undoubtedly survive. An alternative is to tie up some flies on thin-wired, barbless hooks; with 20-pound test you can easily straighten these right out rather than break them off, and that's better for the fish.

Once at boatside the traditional method has been to lip gaff the fish, then haul it partially out of the water for photos. More guides are now keeping the fish in the water and handling it with a pair of gloves to improve their grip. How many photos can we really use? It may not be fatal to most fish, but it can't help them to run a gaff through their mouth tissue and haul them into the air when they are exhausted and in need of oxygen.

Key West, despite its location at the end of the chain, is not hard to reach. A moderate-sized airport provides Key West with jet service from several locations. Key West is a well-developed resort, offering a good number of hotels and some excellent restaurants. During tarpon season, not only do the local guides work the Marquesas and areas west of Key West, but guides from throughout the Keys trailer down to Key West for the prime-time fishing. In my experience, seeing, casting to, hooking, and then experiencing the fight of a big tarpon on a fly rod is the single most exciting fishing experience available to the fly-rod angler.

Chapter
11

Snook—
Chokoloskee,
Florida

*E*ach of the best saltwater fly-fishing locations is a unique place. Experiencing these places is one of the finest rewards of this activity. Few river entrances are as dramatic as the Kennebec's. Fishing there for striped bass is an exhilarating visual experience: framed by the broad sweeps of Popham beach to the west and the fishing village at Bay Point to the east, the mighty river rushes past the weathered, windswept rise of Pond Island toward Seguin Island, dominated by one of the most famous lighthouses on the entire East Coast. Spend a half day casting to surfacing schools of stripers and you will remember the place for a lifetime.

The same can be said of the dramatic islands, bays, rips, and beaches of Massachusetts—Martha's Vineyard, Nantucket, the Elizabeths, and the vast reach of Cape Cod. Yes, these are also unforgettable. But are they any more so than the sight of Montauk Light perched on top of its cliff at Long Island's rockbound outermost point, a place where the tide's constant turbulence provides the Atlantic's finned predators with one of their finest feeding grounds? Just one visit to those eternally tossing waters "under the light" at Montauk is sure to take its permanent place in your finest fishing memories.

The images persist as you move south: the wonderful panoramas of Barnegat Bay and the incredible expanse of the beaches of the Jersey coast, the mystery and wonder of the Outer Banks of North Carolina. . . . It is surely one measure of saltwater fishing's worthiness that each remarkable venue is a place of such essential purity, a place that forever puts its mark on your consciousness.

Yet, as if to prove the point beyond any challenge, still farther south are Florida's Keys and the exceptional expanse of the largest marine sanctuary on the planet. Drifting silent among the mangroves, gliding across aquamarine flats on spans of clear water no more than knee deep for thousands of square miles, you have to wonder if there is any more visually dramatic seascape anywhere within a mortal's reach.

The answer is yes. For no matter how stunning the surroundings—and they are splendid indeed—that grace the angler's world from Maine to Florida, none is more superlative, more mysterious, more breathtaking, and more unforgettable than the glorious maze of meadows and marshes, freshwater and saltwater, mangroves and tidal rivers, hummocks and floating islands that stretches from Cape Sable to Fort Myers: the region of the Everglades known as Ten Thousand Islands, surely one of the most fascinating, last purely wild places in the continental United States.

And wonder of wonders, it is one of the most productive places on the globe to cast your fly for snook—that uniquely south Florida fish of dark waters and mangroves. But then snook are just one of the several sporting species that favor this wild and mysterious region. There are tarpon, large and small, mangrove snapper, redfish, and more. You have a good chance of meeting both alligators and crocodiles, manatees, many kinds of crabs, spiny lobster, frogs, mangrove terrapin, and formidable rattlesnakes. This complex intersection of saltwater and freshwater, land and sea, marsh and mangrove is a true jungle, quite untamed, some of it still uncharted, and all of it teeming with multitudes of every natural presence except humankind, of which there are still relatively few.

"Until the second half of the nineteenth century," writes my friend Peter Matthiessen in *Killing Mr. Watson,* his excellent novel set in the heart of the region,

> the southern half of the Florida peninsula, and in particular, its far southwestern region, was scarcely known. This rainy and mosquito-ridden labyrinth of mangrove islands and dark tidal rivers was all but uninhabited, despite its marvelous abundance of fish and game. "The Ten Thousand Islands," as one naturalist has written, "is a region of mystery and loneliness: gloomy, monotonous, weird, and strange, yet possessing a decided fascination. To the casual stranger each and every part of the region looks exactly like the rest; each islet and water passage seems but the counterpart of hundreds of others. Even those familiar with its tortuous channels often get lost, wandering for days among its labyrinthine ways."
>
> Of the thousands of islands, less than a hundred—mostly in the north—rise more than one foot above sea level, and on most of these the high ground is

too limited to build upon: the more or less habitable barrier islands include perhaps 30 on the Gulf with sand banks up to six feet high and about 40 hammock islands farther inland.

On these, as a precaution against hurricanes, the Calusa Indians constructed substantial shell mounds—or, more properly, hilly ridges—up to 20 feet in height, on which pockets of soil suitable for farming have accumulated. There were also extensive mainland mounds at Turner River that were later farmed by Chokoloskee pioneers.

And speaking of pioneers, few 19th century anglers were more adventurous (and few have been since) than Anthony W. Dimock, the New York financier who made a great deal of money in a relatively short time and then spent most of the rest of his days fly fishing south Florida waters, primarily for tarpon. He caught his first in February 1882, and went on from there to catch hundreds more, most of which he released. And that was almost a century before hook-and-release fishing became the norm.

A.W. Dimock (as he signed himself) also caught his share of snook, for he was a true angler who loved every aspect of the sport. He was also a pioneer, an explorer who gave scarcely a thought to navigating the breadth of what is now Everglades National Park, from Everglades City on what is now the park's western border east to Miami at the edge of the Atlantic. The year was 1907, and Dimock, his son, a friend, and an Indian guide named Tommy Osceola made the trip in two small boats—a canoe and an outboard-powered launch. It is difficult these days to visualize the engine that propelled what Dimock called a power boat. But believe me, it was very different from today's dependable outboards equipped with computerized ignition systems and automatic fuel injection. And the Ten Thousand Islands territory that Dimock and his companions traversed with nothing more than a compass and dead reckoning was unexplored, uncharted, and largely unknown except to the Indians who lived in its lush interior.

When the six-day trip was over, this remarkable man described it this way: "Crossing the Everglades in a canoe is not an adventure, it is a picnic."

Perhaps, but his journal describes what most of us would consider a bit more arduous than a picnic. Describing the trip's fourth day, Dimock writes,

The next day we were in the water a good deal. The motor boat had to be pushed and hauled. The open water, which we followed when possible, often led so far from our course that we had to drag our boats over water that was shoal and ran through grass that tugged against us. A bit of dry land was secured for a midday camp by blowing the head off a cottonmouth moccasin which had pre-empted it. We discovered in the afternoon a beautiful camping ground of Indian antecedents, half-an-acre in extent, dry, level as a floor, covered with pawpaws and fringed with wild grapes and cocoa-plums. Piles of shells of turtles and snail, bones of deer, and remnants of fish told how life might be maintained in the Glades. That afternoon, our course was guided by the dead top of a tall mastic-tree, at the foot of which was an Indian camp with the fire still burning.

We camped beside it among pumpkin vines, and ate roasted taniers and pumpkins which we gathered from the little field where grew oranges, bananas, corn and sugar cane. The songs of birds awakened me in the morning, and I recognized cardinal, king, and mocking birds, and saw one horned owl, several black hawks and many crows.

There's more, much more, but as you can tell from this brief passage, Anthony W. Dimock and the unidentified naturalist quoted by Peter Matthiessen reacted to the Everglades and Ten Thousand Islands in very different ways. Dimock is surely delighted to be exploring; the naturalist is just as convinced the Glades are gloomy.

The difference, I would argue, is that Dimock is an angler, and a fly fisher as well. As a contemporary fly-fishing visitor to Marco Island, Everglades City, and Chokoloskee, I am confident that most of you who take your fly rods in hand and travel to the Ten Thousand Islands in search of snook will see that wonderfully different and special place much as Dimock did, with delight, amazement, and not a little awe.

I waited more than 50 years between the day I saw my first snook and the day I first cast a fly to another. I was 19 in 1942 and going through the final stages of combat flight training aboard an Army Air Corps B-17, better known, and properly so, as a Flying Fortress. We trained at an air base in Avon Park, near Lake Wales in central Florida. But I had friends on Jupiter Island on the Atlantic coast about 20 miles north of Palm Beach, and I hitchhiked across Alligator Alley to visit them whenever I could wrangle a pass.

On the west, inshore, side of Jupiter where the Indian River runs dark and clear, there was (and I'm sure still is) a substantial dock, able to accommodate a good number of some of the grandest yachts that cruised the inland waterway. I discovered my first snook beneath that dock and was fascinated by their attitude. Unlike every fish I had seen before, these large, dark shapes, suspended there as still as stone in those emerald waters, seemed quite unafraid. They could not help seeing me lean far out over the dock's edge, yet they seldom moved. When they did, it was in extraslow motion, without perceptible effort.

I carried their image with me through the war and beyond, but as the years passed, I began believing that those basalt shapes in the dock's dark shadows may have been a mirage, an invention of my active imagination sustained and enhanced over the decades. Some 40 years later my doubts were resolved, this time at Marco Island at the northern end of the Ten Thousand Islands. I arrived as a participant in an informal symposium on the benefits and disbenefits of a proposed real estate development. (I was there as the token environmentalist.) Strolling on the dock at the local marina, I looked down to see the same vision I had carried since 1942—a great log of a snook suspended in the dock's dark shadows.

Only this time I was in a position to arrange for a more intimate meeting. Prevailing on my hosts, I lined up a boat and a skipper who said he could spare an hour or so. We headed south along the inshore edge of the island where a tidal river flows toward Gullivan Bay. I cast a series of streamers toward the mangrove roots that lined the banks—a series because those casts so often ended up hopelessly snarled among the mangroves—but I found no takers, even though we saw what we thought were one or two snook splashing in the mangrove's dark shadows.

More than a decade later, and more than a half century after our first meeting on Jupiter, I arrived at Everglades City in the heart of the Ten Thousand Islands, at the epicenter of what is surely Florida's finest snook habitat. If you drive southeast along the only road from the airport at Fort Myers, you spend much of your journey with the Everglades on both sides. If you look sharply enough as you cross over the myriad creeks, sloughs, and canals, you'll surely see an alligator. Quite suddenly, the road leaves its sea of green behind as you enter the outskirts of a small community looking as if it wants to be much larger, much grander.

Your entrance becomes a broad, divided boulevard fit for a metropolis, lined with arched, wrought-iron street lights. When you arrive at a grand and imposing traffic circle, you realize that this thoroughfare was designed and built for a small city, yet the boulevard is bordered only by palm trees and a few modest frame houses. Evidently, someone once had a master plan for making Everglades City the Miami of Florida's southwest coast.

That someone was Barron Collier, a contemporary and fellow millionaire of Anthony Dimock, who followed that pioneer to the Everglades and built the Rod and Gun Club on the banks of the Collier River in 1899. Collier built it as a sample of how the grand manner could be brought to the wilds of south Florida, provided it could be built before the income tax. With its wonderfully high ceilings, its ancient paddle fans, its now rather threadbare mounted tarpon, snook, and redfish, all enclosed by spacious function rooms paneled in dark cypress, the Rod and Gun Club is the last vestige of those backwoods glory days, those days when Collier greeted U.S. presidents, Barrymores, and even Gypsy Rose Lee as members and guests arriving for a few days' fishing.

This is a place with an angling history that spans more than a century, a grand dame of a place set down amidst some of the nation's most untamed wilderness, a literal jungle that crowds against the small settlement's modest homes, stores, and several restaurants that hand their patrons some of the most exotic and varied menus in all of Florida. You can, if you are adventurous, order gator tail, rattlesnake steaks, black-tip shark fillets, grilled pompano, frogs' legs, stone crabs, Gulf shrimp, oysters by the dozen, and a Florida staple, key lime pie, for dessert.

Chokoloskee, the centerpiece settlement of *Killing Mr. Watson*, is just a few miles down the road. It is another place with a wild and woolly history that goes back more than a century. It is also where Capt. Gil Drake, one of the world's best fishing guides, now has a second home. Several years ago, feeling the pressure of the increasing hundreds of thousands of visitors to Key West, and the thousands of newly arrived anglers, Gil came to Chokoloskee and began exploring those hundreds of miles of unexplored waters among the Ten Thousand Islands. With his sixth sense for fish and their favorite habitats and his incredible eye for detail, he has already learned more than most of us will ever know about where to find snook that have never before seen a fly. Unlike those seasoned veterans under the docks at Jupiter and Marco, these are wild snook who live in the wildest of waters.

In previous chapters, we have avoided recommending specific guides, primarily because there are so many good ones out there and because there are always new good ones launching boats at the start of their careers. But Capt. Gil Drake is an exception, as even his most worthy competitors will agree. He is a guide who loves the mysterious waters of Ten Thousand Islands and the remarkable number of fish that live in them. So if you are making your first trip for snook and tarpon in the Glades, it's worth the effort to locate Gil (either in Key West or Chokoloskee) and to give him a call. It's best if you make that call about a year ahead. But hey, give it a shot. You never know. He may have a cancellation, although that almost never happens.

As someone who has been seeing snook in my mind's eye for more than a half century now, I can promise you that you won't have to wait nearly that long to meet yours if you start almost anywhere on the waters of the Ten Thousand Islands. Don't forget, however, that these are the wildest waters in the nation. If you try traveling them alone, you're sure to get yourself lost. But as A.W. Dimock tells us, not to worry; after a day or two, you'll most likely find your way home.

Tackle and Techniques

When I was a boy growing up in Friendship, Maine, my grandparents gave me a subscription to *Outdoor Life* that they continued to renew through my college years. I read many issues from cover to cover, especially the fishing stories. Among the species that were commonly written about was snook. I was especially attracted to snook, since its shape and love of the nighttime surf reminded me of New England's striped bass. The fish are of comparable size, although the stripers grow a bit bigger. Snook have large fins, a moderately compressed body side to side, and a prominent, thin black line down their green and silver sides that makes them easy to identify positively. They're no relative of the bass, though, and in fact they look similar to a tarpon. A small, related fish called a tarpon-snook looks very much like a cross between the two fish, and it accentuates how similar looking tarpon and snook are, even though I believe that they're in no way related. In the late '50s, snook were quite plentiful in Florida. During the '70s and early '80s, however, the population was depleted, largely through commercial fishing. Florida made the snook a game fish and regulated it with strict management measures; now the snook population is back at healthy levels.

Snook are warm-water fish, and when water temperatures drop much below 60 degrees, which can happen during extreme winter freezes in the shallow waters favored by snook, it's not unusual for wholesale deaths to occur. This has happened in some areas, and population recovery takes years. Needless to say, snook are far more common in the southern half of Florida, especially in the vast area where the Everglades dump into the Gulf of Mexico. Unlike stripers, snook are not anadromous fish, but neither are they a pelagic species. Spawning takes place during the summer months, and in saltwater, but not far from shore. The eggs require both saltwater and flowing water to be viable. Snook are thought to be hermaphroditic; almost all younger fish are males, and older ones females. Except when spawning, though, snook show no aversion to freshwater. In fact, snook, and some large ones at that, are frequently found far back in the Everglades, in essentially freshwater habitat. The same is true in some of the chocolate-colored, Central American freshwater rivers that have produced many of the record snook. Areas without significant freshwater influence, like the lower Keys, have almost no snook population.

The record in Florida, though less than the 53-pound Costa Rican fish, is a respectable 44 pounds, and there are thought to be many fish larger than that along the mangrove-rimmed shorelines of southern Florida. It may be, in large part, the snook's frequenting of these brackish-water areas that keeps the Florida record from being broken. My old friend Brock Apfel fishes near Punta Gorda, Florida. Brock's tunnel-hulled johnboat allows him access to the brackish-water backcountry near his home, which holds plenty of big snook. Brock tells me that you can see them, lying here and there like logs out in front of the mangroves, but that they are as wary as a black duck during open season. If by some miracle you do hook one, the thing heads through a minefield of old logs and stumps before finally disappearing into the oyster-encrusted roots of the mangroves, from which you're unlikely to extract them. Joe Brooks, in his 1957 book *Greatest Fishing*, recounts a snook trip to an Everglades lake, in an area called New River, just south of the Tamiami Trail. " 'Biggest one yet,' yelled Otto. 'About fifteen pounds. . . . Give him the butt. . . .' Then that fish decided to go for the mangroves,

200 feet away. He made it in one run. . . . He's deep in the roots! . . . Then we heard shouts from the shore. All three of them—Doc, Otto, and John—were standing in the skiff and Leldon was out on the mangrove roots. . . . Leldon went across the roots and turned him this way. We watched, fascinated, as inch by inch the fish came out." At one point during Brooks' trip back into the Everglades, their boat hit a submerged log, and the outboard motor was ripped completely off the boat. Such are the antics that may be involved with landing a big snook in the Everglades.

It's not just snags that can make snook tough to land. Besides being strong as bulls, snook have three other excellent defenses. First, snook have gill covers like razor blades. The sharp edges can easily cut your hand or a taut piece of monofilament leader. Second, snook are terrific jumpers. Besides all the things that can happen to you with any jumping fish, snook can literally jump into overhanging branches, tangling you and then breaking you off. Third, snook, like tarpon, have a very raspy mouth. I've caught small snook, on 20-pound-test bite tippets, that nearly ground right through the line during a five-minute fight. The mouth of a snook is so raspy that you should wear gloves before sticking your thumb in there.

Snook eat most of the typical Florida Bay fare available to them. Crabs, shrimp, and small fish of every kind—the live-bait fishers' prize pinfish and mullet—are among their favorite forage. I once read that the famous Jimmy Albright—yes, the inventor of the knot—drove the Tamiami Trail on rainy nights; wherever large quantities of frogs were killed in the road he stopped and fished the roadside canal. The cars never got all those frogs, and the snook waited next to the shore to catch the survivors as they jumped into the water. Now there's a versatile feeder. This means that snook will hit everything from the top to the bottom of the shallow water column that they inhabit. When you think about just how shallow the snook's common lies really are, it's not surprising. Snook, as the frog story points out, are big on night feeding. Throughout Florida large snook are frequently taken in the nighttime surf and in the moving waters of inlets. But the dark waters of upper Florida Bay promote daytime feeding from even the nighttime-loving snook. It's a good thing too, because the Lord himself wouldn't go into the Everglades at night unless he had to.

Of all the snook-inhabited waters of southern Florida, among the most productive of all is a vast western area of Everglades National Park called Ten Thousand Islands. Like the rest of the park, Ten Thousand Islands benefits from the nutrient-laden, freshwater flowage that gradually becomes brackish and then salt. But because the area empties more directly into the Gulf of Mexico than does Florida Bay—which is constrained by Florida's mainland on one side, the Keys on the other, and numerous shoals in the middle—the freshwater environment doesn't extend as far seaward as it does in Florida Bay. The transition from Big Cypress Swamp to the tidewater sections of Ten

Thousand Islands starts in the hammock-embroidered, half-land, half-water, sawgrass prairies that gradually evolve into mangrove forests laced with bays and rivers. Finally, the backcountry drains through oyster-bar-edged cuts, until at last the horizon clears to reveal the stunning blue waters of the open Gulf. Rounding that last point of mangroves and suddenly confronting the Gulf's dazzling panorama is always a special part of any fishing trip to this area. I'm left without adequate words to describe the majesty of the open, seemingly limitless horizons that greets the angler emerging from the virtual jungle of the Everglades. The shallow, tropically warm, brackish waters of this area are a superb biological factory. The smell of the decaying nutrients rising from the mucky bottom suggests the incredible fecundity of this place. Schools of mullet jump on the surface, wading birds of all descriptions line the shores, and snook, tarpon, redfish, and sharks bask in the bays or patrol the mangrove shorelines.

This is not a place that I would want to fish on my own without a lot of cautious study. It can be done; people trailer their boats into Everglades City and launch them all the time. And it's not unusual for the park rangers to find them and lead them out a day or two later, reduced by the unbearable heat and clouds of mosquitoes to sweaty, dehydrated, enfeebled shadows of their former selves. I've always thought of myself as at least average in my ability to find my way around, but within a few minutes of winding through the mangrove maze, I haven't the foggiest idea of how to get back where I started. One day, after eight hours of fishing, I stowed my tackle for a long ride back to the marina. Within a minute or less we turned a corner in the mangroves, and the observation tower near our starting point revealed itself to be only a few minutes away, in the direction completely opposite what I had imagined. Thankfully, our guide, a native of the area, knew the islands like the back of his hand.

The fishing day at Ten Thousand Islands often starts with the guides employing the early morning light to pole their flats boats along the shallow mangrove shores. At that time it's difficult to see the fish, so we cast sidearm, skipping our flies toward likely looking spots under the edges of the mangroves. This is where many of the snook live. From under overhanging foliage or at points extending into the constant flow of currents either in or out of the Everglades, we often found snook ranging from four or five pounds on up to double digits in weight. Most of the strikes came within a few feet of the mangrove's cover. Sometimes snook are found in the various holes throughout the flats; these holes are thought to be created by eroded limestone deposits. The darkness of the deeper water of the holes gives fish a bit of camouflage and security. The angler has no choice but to blind cast into the holes. Occasionally we saw a big snook laid up, basking tarponesque on the sunny surface of a dark-watered lagoon. According to our guide these solitary, larger fish are hard to approach in open water, and they'll seldom take a fly. That was our experience, although we saw some fish that looked to be nearly four feet long.

As the sun rises so does your ability to see the redfish and occasionally the snook in the shallows around the mangroves. This made the fishing more interesting, especially for the reds, which don't mind being exposed in shallow water. The snook, though, seemed to move even deeper back into the recesses of the mangroves. Productive casts had to reach back under branches into holes in the mangroves. The better you could execute this kind of low-angled cast, the more frequently you'd hook up. During the day we were constantly laughing at the highly audible antics of snook crashing away at baitfish far back in the cover of the mangroves.

The typical first inclination of these fish, once hooked, is to jump, and surprisingly high. The second is to make a beeline back toward the roots of the mangroves. Once in there, it's all over, so the need to stop their retreat is paramount. Although the fish in open water could be easily handled on a seven- or eight-weight rod, I suggest at least a nine to have the backbone to haul a decent snook out of cover. Because the water is so dark, a long leader is unnecessary. You should, though, tie a foot-long length of 30-pound test to the 15 at the end of your tapered leader to handle the abrasive mouth of the snook. You won't need a large reel because few of the fish caught in this setting will head for open water and make any long runs. It will be necessary, though, to pull like the devil on them, using the extreme butt of the rod to keep a big one from getting into the roots of the mangroves. Much of this water is very shallow, so a floating line is usually best. Because snook are so wary, the greater the distance from which you make a presentation the better. Placement under the mangrove branches is critical; therefore, I recommend working a fly line with a long head, which will yield increases in both control and distance. A line with a long head requires more false casting to make each presentation, but these fish aren't going anywhere unless you scare them. Along the edges of some of the passes a sink tip, or something like a 250-grain shooting head, will come in handy. I'd bring a second rod already set up, because you may go back and forth between these types of structures.

Many snook are taken on popping bugs, but I'm not a fan of poppers. Fish tend to try to swallow everything in the area when attacking a popper, because they can't see exactly where it is. Many fish are therefore hooked in the back of the throat or the gills. These are high mortality places to hook fish, and removing the hook is difficult because the body of the popper may block your view of the hook's location. Poppers are also easily hung up in the limbs of the mangroves and are more difficult to cast. Similarly, bottom-tending flies like the Clouser or various crab flies face another set of problems. The first of these is that the snook, unlike a redfish or bonefish, does not have an underslung or inferior mouth; bottom grubbing is not their natural tendency. From a more practical view, though, the oozy bottom of the Ten Thousand Islands area is a magnet for flies. Writers discussing bonefishing describe the crab pattern emerging from a little puff of sand. A weighted fly that goes to the bottom off Everglades City is likely to emerge in a cloud of black crud, and then only after a yank that might pull it six feet along the bottom. A snook would likely think it was being attacked! The best flies for this fishing seem to be weedless minnow imitations, tied about two or three inches long. Brock Apfel, fishing near his Punta Gorda home waters, often prefers a muddler minnow. The spun-hair head of the muddler moves a bit more water than will a fly with a thin head, and, depending on how it's trimmed, it can be retrieved right in the surface film, adding the feature of partial obscurity to its appeal. On my first trip to Ten Thousand Islands Brock had supplied us both with one of his favorite flies, a lime green bend-back (see figure 11.1). This fly—composed of a bit of bucktail, a couple of grizzly hackles, and sometimes a bit of flash material, all tied in at the head of the fly—is a good, generic simulation of many of the countless species of small baitfish in the Everglades. Although one can buy the hooks to make a bend back, Brock bent his own (see figure 11.2). This design has two advantages. First, it is weedless, a feature that can also be accomplished with a mono-filament weed guard. Second, because of the bend back, it rides with the hook up so that it won't foul on the bottom. We cast Brock's flies far up under the mangroves and caught many snook, seldom losing a fly.

The home base for this fishery is a little outpost of a town called Everglades City. Here the homes are built on stilts, in anticipation of the next big hurricane. This is a laid-back place, a perfect fishing destination. As the Everglades Rod and Gun Club can attest, it has been so for more than a century. Here is a place, with traditional dark mahogany matched-board ceilings and a huge riverfront screened-in porch off the dining room, where anglers, weary of battling tarpon and snook, can relax, protected from the mosquitoes, after a day under the southern Florida sun. Last time I stayed there, the reservations were simply written in a book, no deposit requested. Hemingway

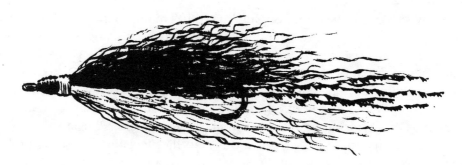

Figure 11.1 *Bend-back fly.*

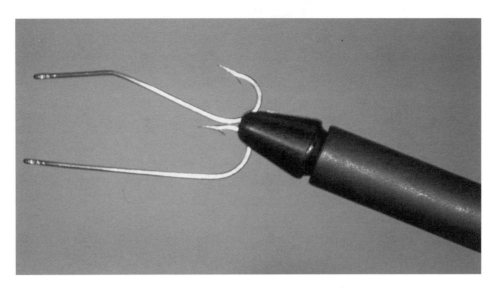

Figure 11.2 *The hook on the top has been modified to tie a bend-back fly on.*

staggered up these stairs, and undoubtedly fished some of the waters that you will if you go to Ten Thousand Islands.

Thanks to better fisheries management than is practiced in much of the country, Florida has excellent fishing, and it's in demand, especially from northerners like me who tire of ice and snow. This demand produces an ample selection of knowledgeable local guides. A small marina at a nearby store is home to several of these guides; others trailer in and launch there or at the nearby village of Chokoloskee. There is excellent fishing in Ten Thousand Islands year round, but the dead of winter can supply cold fronts that temporarily chill the waters beyond the liking of these temperature-sensitive fish.

To fish Ten Thousand Islands, you can fly into a number of places, including Fort Myers, which has a good-sized airport with a supply of rental cars. If the Rod and Gun Club is full, the nearby Naples area has a great supply of lodging and restaurants.

Chapter
12

Redfish—
Port O'Connor,
Texas

O ver the years, I've been called a lucky man countless times—so many times that I have long since stopped thinking of it as a compliment. It happens most often with dinner guests. After a guest has dined on one of Jean's delicious meals, he will turn to me and ask, "Do you eat like this every night?" And when I say yes, knowing what's coming next, the guy will shake his head and tell me, "Boy, are you a lucky man."

Often, it doesn't take a dinner. Many men have looked at Jean, then at me, and then back at Jean again. And here it comes: "Boy, are you a lucky man." What they are really saying, of course, is that I don't deserve such a lovely, patient, soft-spoken, and (in the eyes of too many observers) long-suffering wife. Most folks consider my irresponsibility, my financial anemia, and my general impatience as good reasons for a life of eternal discomfort, canned food, and loneliness that, by rights, should be the unavoidable penalty for a disposition as rancid as mine.

So, sensing they are in contact with a fellow who has gotten away with figurative murder and evidently will continue to do so, they come up with, "Boy, are you a lucky man," as a way of making certain I know they consider me quite undeserving of any of the several magnificent presences that make my life such a splendid adventure.

It's been more than a half century now since folks started telling me how lucky I am. You'd think 50 years of this oblique put-down might get to a guy, but hey, I'm resilient. Besides, the guys are right, although in my opinion it's not good manners on their part to keep reminding me that dumb luck is the only reason I've made it this far.

When it comes to my friend John Graves, I must say I do know how lucky I am. If it weren't for John, I'd still be wandering through life with all the misconceptions of Texas that most of us easterners seem compelled to cling to. And I'll have to give much of the credit for my good luck to my sister, Jane, who had the stubbornness, loyalty, and raw courage to marry John and move to Texas with him, in spite of some of the most determined maternal opposition you can imagine. If you had seen our mother at the Manhattan cocktail party at which John was officially introduced to his fiancee's family and some of her Social Register friends, you would have gotten just an inkling of the parental dismay over the tragedy of a Yankee young lady (just recently introduced to society at great parental expense) about to run off with a Texan! Why, it was more than even indulgent parents could reasonably be expected to countenance, and our parents were not known for their indulgence, believe me.

Add to that the reports that John Graves had no respectable occupation. He was then, and still is, a writer. When I once told my father that I wanted to be a writer, he said, "But John, you can't even spell," and gave me a dictionary to prove it. And here was a "writer" from Texas, which in the East in those days was a classic contradiction in terms. It is one measure, among many, of John's grit and patient forbearance that he endured that entire wedding and its attendant occasions with such obdurate dignity.

It was years, however, before I got to know him. First, some 30 years after that remarkable wedding, Jean and I visited John and Jane at their ranch in Glen Rose, a town smaller than a New York City block about 30 miles southwest of Fort Worth. Definitely a small ranch, the place is well delineated by John in his book *Hardscrabble,* which, for a one-word title, pretty much describes the scrubby limestone-ledge country that surrounds the house that John and Jane built themselves. On one of those visits, we walked the ranch to what Texans call a tank, which is a hole they've scooped in the ground to hold water for the few cattle that can find a living on the open range. We caught catfish in the tank and over a wonderful dinner of fresh catfish fillets fried in cornmeal, John and I talked about how much we both loved fishing.

That event led to annual visits by John and Jane to Key West during the years Jean and I lived there. Those visits averaged a month or six weeks, and we spent most of our time on the flats, fishing for tarpon, barracuda, and gray snapper. The snapper met the same delightful fate as those catfish from the tank.

Among many other fields of interest John Graves lists fly fishing near the top, and it was from him that I learned just about everything that's important about this many-splendored activity. Like everything he does, John fly fishes with a sense of the sport's perfection. He has researched rods, reels, flies, and fly tying. He designed and built his flats skiff and taught himself to pole it in a straight line. And if you think that's a simple skill, easily acquired, then I suggest you try it.

John also makes a point of collecting information about wind, tides, and water temperatures. He analyzes the relationship of each with the other and the likelihood that the combination might be favorable to a fly caster. This is a man who misses almost every time when he tries to spit tobacco juice over the gunwale but who is meticulous when it comes to researching the feeding habits of the gray snapper in the waters off the lower Keys.

The same, however, cannot be said of my sister Jane, who was then and still is John's companion on almost every fishing trip. Sweet sister Jane. She tries, she really does. But, if I can put it kindly, she is a much better wife and mother than angler. This has led to some amusing moments on the water. Most recently she and John were both casting their respective flies, she from the bow of John's skiff, John from the stern. Jane fell over-board from her perch on the bow. John was concentrating so intently on working the chartreuse Clouser he had tied that he remained quite un-aware of his wife's immersion. At last she floated past him just off the stern. "Jane," asked a perplexed John, "What the hell are you doing back here?"

Much like his brother-in-law, John has made many good friends in the fly-fishing community, some of whom are kind enough to take him and Jane to some of the finest fishing waters on the globe. Foremost among those friends is Robert McCurdy of Bastrop, another modest mid-Texas town. Like John, Robert is a writer; unlike John, he spent a few years as a professional fishing guide and knows more than most about where to find redfish along the 360 miles of the Texas Gulf coast. He has, on numerous occasions, taken John and Jane on redfish expeditions, and, at least once, guided Jane to his favorite spots—of which more later.

After nearly a half century of stalking redfish in the shallows behind the Texas barrier beaches that embroider the coast from Port Arthur to Padre Island, Robert has chosen a broad-beamed, 20-foot canoe as the most suit-able craft. "It's very stable," he explains, "almost impossible to capsize. And I can pole it in just a few inches of water.

"There is plenty of room for both John and Jane. They were with me this fall when we fished some shallows near Port Aransas. I've seen a great many redfish over the years, but I don't think I've seen more of them in one place than we did that morning. Jane was casting about once a minute. John was more deliberate—he cast about every three minutes. Jane hooked up with a big red, 30 inches or better, and that fish took off.

"John had rigged Jane's rod with a direct-drive reel, and Jane beat up her knuckles pretty good when that big fish began its run. I noticed John had a nice, new antireverse reel, so I asked him why Jane was working with such an old model. John said, 'I know it's old, but I just love the sound it makes when there's a big fish running off line. Don't you just love that sound?'

"I suggested that John could hear that old reel better if it was on his rod, but I didn't get very far with that idea.

"A few days later, I went fishing with Jane. John was working on some article he had to finish. There weren't quite as many redfish as there had been that other day, but there were plenty to keep us occupied.

"Jane was in the bow, casting. I thought I'd step out of the canoe for just a few minutes and try wading to another bunch of fish just a short ways behind us. Well, I hadn't taken more than a few steps when I looked back to see how Jane was doing. For some reason I'll never understand, she'd started leaning back over the gunwale. I told myself she won't lean much further. She surely knows better.

"But she just kept leaning. Maybe she thought she needed to lean as far as she could to make a longer cast. I'll never know. But in another second or two she'd leaned far enough to tip that canoe right over, and I'm telling you, that canoe is as stable as they get.

"What a mess. Everything spilled into the mud, including Jane. That rod and reel was so covered with mud it looked like some strange sort of flower bulb, just a bulge where the reel should be. I had to scrape that mud off everything, like scraping at soft butter with a dull knife. Jane had mud in her hair, mud all over her face, all over everything.

"It took a while, but we eventually got back to fishing again. And those redfish were still around. I didn't mind all that much. But I still don't understand how or why Jane did that. I mean, it takes a lot to tip over that canoe. But Jane never seemed to mind all that much. She's a game girl. A great girl. And I'll tell you something, I never have liked smart women all that much anyway."

Like everyone who has fly fished the Texas coast for as long as he has, Robert McCurdy will tell you the fishing has never been better. "I grew up here, and I started fishing when I was 9. Next month I'll be 50, and I've never seen as many redfish as I've seen over the past several years. I'm not saying you have to capsize your canoe to prove it. But even if you do, the fish will still be there once you put everything to rights."

Tackle and Techniques

For as long as I can remember, and undoubtedly for a long time before that, anglers have been drawing parallels between the channel bass and the striped bass. Of the three common names the channel bass goes by, I picked the name most similar to the striper's, just to reinforce this notion. Perhaps I'm dating myself a bit with the name channel bass. I've really not heard it used in eons. The more common names today are red drum or just plain redfish. In any case, the redfish might well be described as the southern equivalent of the striper, not so much by its biology but by its megavalue to inshore recreational fishing. The body shape, fins and face excepting, is much like the striper, as is the range of sizes it attains. Certainly the redfish is colored differently, most of its body being a copper shade of red, darker on top than the bottom, although some fish take on an almost greenish appearance. Instead of stripes, the redfish has spots, maybe as few as one, maybe several, but at least one large, black spot back beside its tail. This is undoubtedly a false eye, picked up somewhere in the redfish's evolution to confuse predators about which way their hoped-for meal was heading. This spot has become a hallmark, prominently displayed beside the glistening tail in countless paintings and photographs of a redfish standing on its head as it grubs in the bottom. This too is a major difference between the striper and the redfish. Although a striper occasionally may be found tailing, it's standard practice for the redfish. This is because the redfish has the inferior, underslung mouth, possessed by only one other fish in this book, the bonefish. It is not, however, as suckerish in design as that of the bonefish. The redfish, despite the difficulties its mouth must cause it, is happy to feed on the surface.

The range of the redfish is extensive; though probably due to overfishing, it's rare north of the Chesapeake, where years ago it was more common. The redfish of the upper East Coast are more migratory than the southern fish because redfish are not a cold-water fish and must return to warmer water during the winter. In the South, however, redfish populations do not make extensive migrations, though some individual fish exhibit wanderlust. Redfish are common along both coasts of Florida—though the east coast seems to hold much larger fish—and all along the states that border the Gulf of Mexico. They seem to like being near supplies of brackish water, so although they are numerous around the Everglades, they are not found very far out on the Keys.

Redfish start spawning at about four years of age, when they are approximately 28 inches long. Off the Texas coast, which will be the center of our discussion, redfish spawn in the surf, near the passes. A pass is a Texas term for inlet, a slot in the barrier islands that leads to the back bays lining the Texas coast. Redfish spawn in September and October, a time of year that, perhaps as part of nature's plan, coincides with hurricane season. The young redfish, complete with several days' food in their yolk sacs, are washed through the passes into the bays. Inside the bays, the young redfish grow quickly in the warm, nutrient-laden environment. If a hurricane produces new passes through the barrier islands, as they commonly do, a bumper crop of redfish can result. Scientists theorize that the net fisheries of the past may have altered the spawning behavior of the redfish; because all the big redfish that lived inside the bays were caught, only individuals with a genetic predisposition to spawning in the ocean survived. That situation may now be reversing itself; spawning may be taking place directly in the bays. Some think that this will boost the already healthy redfish population.

Redfish are versatile feeders and will eat virtually anything that will fit into their comparatively small mouths. Larger redfish patrol the surf lines for mullet and menhaden, and smaller fish feed in the estuaries and backwaters on the young of the numerous species that thrive in the warm, inshore waters of the Southland. It's sight fishing in the shallow lakes behind the Texas barrier beaches that we'll be focusing on. Redfish are comfortable in shallow water; it's not unusual to find redfish of 30 inches frequenting water that will not completely cover their dorsal fins. This is a feature that helps make them the preferred angling target that they are. Shallow waters allow sight fishing, either from a boat or while wading, and people love this style of fishing, especially for potentially large fish like redfish.

Redfish are strong fish. When you couple this with their shallow-water habitat it means they will run for the sanctuary of deeper water. The runs can therefore be terrific reel spinners. Long runs like these leave a fish that is essentially designed for bulldogging quite exhausted. So you get the best of both worlds—a spectacular fight yet one that allows for a quick landing and a safe release. Not that all redfish are released. A redfish fillet, cooked over open flames, using its skin and scales as a grill, and seasoned with some Cajun seafood mixture is among the most delicious fish that I've ever eaten, and I've eaten lots of fish!

Today's Texas redfish population can support a reasonable personal-use harvest. Thanks to the incredible conservation work of what was formerly the Gulf Coast Conservation Association—it's now the Coastal Conservation Association of Texas—all commercial fishing for redfish was stopped, along with the use of gill nets that might inadvertently kill redfish. The fishery is now a model for inshore fisheries management everywhere; the resource is abundant, and the people who expend the effort to catch the wild fish are the ones who eat them, the way it ought to be everywhere. Today the coast of Texas boasts an enormous recreational fishing industry that provides thousands of times the financial and social value of the obsolete commercial fishery it replaced. One-time gill-net fishermen are now guides, many of whom will not let a sport onto their boat until the angler joins the CCA. Bait and tackle stores abound, myriad boats specially made for shallow-water fishing are manufactured and sold locally, and saltwater license revenues from the burgeoning number of anglers have financed excellent science, access, and enforcement investments. Everyone is benefiting. What many of us would give to have those values injected into some of the eastern seaboard states. Too frequently managers there cling to a set of values that protects the interests of a tiny and constantly decreasing portion of the population at the expense of the general public, both financially and through the depletion of the quality of their lives.

Of all the great redfishing to be found along the coast of Texas, the best may be centered on Port O'Connor. The entire coast has excellent numbers of redfish, but it's the fishing conditions that separate this middle-of-the-coast area from the eastern and southern areas. To the east lie very productive waters, but a significant freshwater flow often makes those inshore waters too turbid for sight fishing. Houston, for example, receives 50 inches of rain a year. To the south, Laguna Madre receives little rain, and its enormous bay is hypersaline. The area around Port O'Connor and Matagorda Bay is a combination of the two environments. Moderate freshwater runoff creates vast spartina grass marshes that stretch in seemingly endless succession along the shorelines; these marshes are filled with wading birds and various wildlife that add immeasurably to an angler's days afield. Even though the area is so biologically productive, it is still saline enough to possess the clear water necessary for sight fishing.

Just outside of Port O'Connor is Cavallo Pass. This is the pass with the big jacks that we referred to at the beginning of the book. On the south side of the pass lies Matagorda Island. The inshore side of the island is a vast honeycomb of interconnected lakes. These are not freshwater lakes but shallow salt or brackish ponds, formed and constantly modified by the effects of storm surge, siltation, plant growth, tides, and wind. It is this network of lakes that makes up the premier sight-fishing territory.

In the area of Port O'Connor itself, the best fishing requires a boat, not necessarily to fish from but to get to the fishy places. My host in Port O'Connor, Walter Fondren, one of the founders and national chairman of the Coastal Conservation Association, has had a lifetime's association with the area and its redfish. Walter fishes from a custom-made, flat-bottomed, ultralow-freeboard, jet-outboard-powered boat. This rig will get up on a plane on wet mud without perceptible elevation of the bow, yet it is 20 feet long. The boat has a tower on the bow from which to cast and one on the stern to pole or fish from. The height gives you a wonderful advantage when looking into the water, though many redfish can still appear too quickly to allow a cast. The distant views that the towers afford over the marshes, bays, and barrier islands are alone worth the boat ride.

Some channels between the lakes are so small that as you pass through them both sides of the boat touch the semisolid shoreline. In some cases, you simply get up a head of steam and leap across bars at the entrances to the back lakes that you could never have otherwise reached. But even this specialty craft isn't always able to navigate the skinny water of the back lakes. Walter is full of stories about himself and another veteran CCA man, Don Perkins, digging, pushing, and winching for hours to extricate their boats from solid groundings.

Sometimes the water levels in the back lakes simply get too low to hold fish, though this is rare. Tides are extremely small, less than a foot, in these back bays. Because of the complex path of the channels and the constrictions along them, the tidal rise and fall in the lakes is almost insignificant, and greatly delayed from the times of high or low tide out in the passes. The effect of the wind is another story. Prolonged periods of wind from one direction or another can cause the water levels to remain constantly higher or lower than normal.

The effects on fishing are surprising. Walter theorizes that because fish like to swim into moving water, a slow flow of current out of the lakes, causing falling water levels, encourages fish to move far back into the lakes. In moving from one lake to another it is not uncommon to see redfish swimming with their backs partially exposed, and some of these redfish may be 30 inches or more in length.

Another interesting nuance concerns wading anglers. The Texas flats offer those fond of wading some sensational fishing opportunities. The sides of the lakes that face inland are in the lee of the prevailing onshore wind; these flats usually offer solid and excellent wading. The sides of the lakes that face the onshore wind are apparently muddier and more subject to erosion, and therefore have both poorer footing and inferior visibility (see figure 12.1). In any case, you need a boat to get to all of these lakes, with one big exception.

The state of Texas Parks Department operates a ferry service from Port O'Connor out to Matagorda Island, landing near Cavallo Pass. Once on the island anglers can either fish the surf—prime for larger redfish, especially during the fall—or walk along the inland side of the island to the lakes. A few precautions are in order. First, stay away from the wrack lines—this is rattlesnake country, and they love piles of debris that can shelter them. Second, as in the Keys, shuffle your feet when wading so you don't step on a stingray. Redfish are a great fish to wade for; it's not unusual, says Walter, to get so close that you can literally dangle your fly from the rod tip onto the fish.

When it comes to flies, it's hard to beat a small popper. Not only do the fish seem to like these as well as or better than any subsurface pattern that's been tried, but the popper keeps you off the weedy bottoms of these lakes. Although there are occasional patches of clear sand, grass of some kind covers most of the bottom, and your fly will inevitably get into it. Interestingly enough, redfish will still hit lures moving through the weeds; they do it all the time with jigs retrieved on bait-casting tackle. It's easy to get your fly snarled in the weeds, though, and certainly not as much fun as watching them take a popper. The biggest problem with using poppers is that the large forehead of the redfish creates a bow wave that pushes the popper aside. Because of its underslung mouth, the fish then often misses the popper. The solution seems to be in using slim, pencil-popper styled flies (see figure 12.2). The longer, thinner shape of these flies allows them to stay more firmly in the path of the

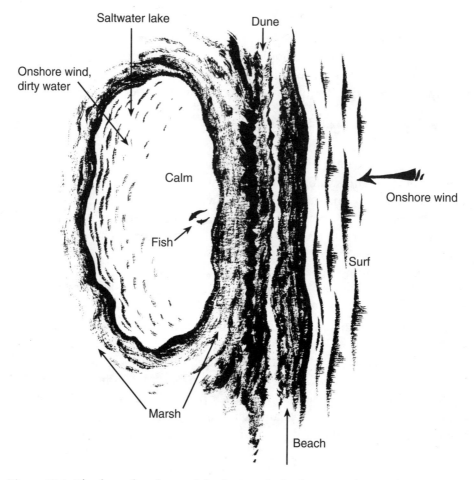

Figure 12.1 *The shore of a saltwater lake that's in the lee from prevailing onshore winds will normally be clearer and hold more fish.*

oncoming redfish. The lakes are a tranquil environment, and even a large redfish is easily spooked by too large a fly, too flashy a fly, or one retrieved too aggressively. A small fly, with no flash material, copper or gold in color, retrieved in short pulls, is just the ticket for success. It's surprising to see tailing fish turn upward and charge a popper, but they'll do it. I've cast a popper in front of a group of tailing redfish and had several of them competing for it.

As in all sight fishing, time is of the essence. Redfish are less nervous than bonefish, move along the flats more slowly, and take more readily, but they won't move any farther out of their way for a fly than will a bonefish. In general, the casts need not be exceptionally long, rarely over 60 feet. Poppers, however, are a bit more difficult to cast than tiny bonefish flies. Generally, I'd say that an eight-weight is about right. If you're an excellent caster, a seven will add to your sport, and a nine gives you more control and power on a windy day—though the fish will usually be closer to you on such a day.

Figure 12.2 *Despite their underslung or "inferior" mouth, redfish love the little poppers.*

Although I've never used a clear floating line, this might be a good application for one. But I've never had a problem catching Texas redfish with garden-variety, weight-forward, solid-colored floating lines. A short head, often prescribed for strong winds, or a very long head, often suggested for extreme distance, will in the first case splash more heavily than desired, and in the second take too long to work out of the guides. The standard 30-foot head has withstood some evolution to achieve the acceptance that it enjoys. One of the benefits of the tower comes when making your presentations: you can cast with your rod pointed low to the water for stealth or take advantage of the height to make a long cast.

Redfishing in Port O'Connor is essentially a year-round proposition, but the shallow-water fishing in the lakes is a bit more seasonal than that. The fish seem to pull out of the lakes during the summer. Walter theorizes that the shrimp run, which is then at peak, pulls them out of the backcountry. In the winter it can simply get too cold for the fish in the ultrashallow water. The best times seem to be during fall and spring.

If you decide to come, you'll be happy to know that although Port O'Connor is a quiet, coastal town, the area has several motels, and—as I can attest—some excellent Gulf seafood restaurants. A number of local launching ramps are available, but as we discussed, you really need one of those extreme shallow-water boats to get the most out of this world-class fishery for redfish. As with some of the other exciting fisheries, it's best to start with a guide. The area around Port O'Connor now boasts a good selection of guides who specialize in fly fishing.

Index

Locators followed by *f* indicate reference to figures.

About the Authors

John N. Cole has spent the last 65 years fishing this nation's saltwaters. He has worked to raise awareness of the environment and various species of fish and was previously named *Outdoor Life's* Conservationist of the Year. Currently a freelance writer for *Outdoor Life* and *Fly Fishing in Saltwaters*, Cole has served as editor of the *Maine Times* and Director of the National Audubon Society. Cole has written 18 books on fishing, birds, and house construction. He currently resides with his wife, Jean, in Brunswick, Maine.

Brad Burns has a deep love for saltwater fly fishing, with 40 years of experience in the sport. With an expertise in fishing equipment, Burns has published several articles on tackle, rods, and flies in such notable publications as *Field and Stream, Fly Rod and Reel, Saltwater Sportsman,* and *Fly Fishing in Saltwaters*. He has also published the highly successful *Fly Fishing for Striped Bass Handbook* for L.L. Bean. A national board member of the Coastal Conservation Association, he and his wife, June, live in Falmouth, Maine.

Prize catches for your fishing library

Respected fly fishing author Art Lee returns to print with the hardcover reissue of his classic work *Fishing Dry Flies for Trout on Rivers and Streams*. This book explains both the essentials and the nuances of fly fishing, fly presentation, casting, and fly tying, and amply covers the often-neglected subject of landing trout. Complementing the instruction are more than 100 richly detailed illustrations, photographs by Kris Lee, and a color insert detailing the dry fly patterns recommended in the book.

Item PLEE0777 • ISBN 0-88011-777-X
$24.95 ($36.95 Canada)

In *Tying and Fishing the Riffling Hitch,* Lee explains the three most common hitch configurations and the pros and cons of using each. He takes great care to describe each detail of this little-known technique so that the millions of salmon fishers and steelheaders in North America and around the world can easily understand and use it effectively. He explains that, when used properly, the Hitch will catch fish in almost any condition—especially when nothing else seems to be working. Forty-two extraordinary color illustrations and 31 photos reveal the most effective way to tie and present the Hitch as well as nine of the author's favorite fly patterns.

Item PLEE0782 • ISBN 0-88011-782-6
$21.95 ($29.95 Canada)

Prices are subject to change.

To place your order, U.S. customers
call TOLL FREE 1-800-747-4457
Customers outside the U.S. place your order using the appropriate
telephone number/address shown in the front of this book.

Lore of Trout Fishing is a collection of Lee's work for Fly Fisherman—the sport's most respected magazine—that takes 40 years of classic, time-tested essays on all aspects of fly fishing for trout and puts them together in one volume. Equal parts information and inspiration, this seamless instructional guide is filled with captivating fishing lessons and tales presented in Art Lee's engaging style. The book contains some never-before-published material and nearly 200 illustrations, including an eight-page, full color insert showing Lee's favorite flies.

Item PLEE0790 • ISBN 0-88011-790-7
$26.95 ($39.95 Canada)

Fishing on Ice is full of details about finding and catching the most popular cold climate fish, including walleye, northern pike, crappie, sunfish, jumbo perch, trout, and a few hardwater exotics. It covers proven ice fishing equipment as well as the latest in clothing, rods, reels, line, tackle, fish houses, electronics, heaters, lights, gas-powered and hand augers, snowmobiles and ATVs, and many other important topics. Whether you're a beginner to the sport or an expert who craves the latest advice on techniques and locations, this book will ensure that your ice fishing experience is comfortable, enjoyable, and—most of all—successful.

Item PVIC0926 • ISBN 0-88011-926-8
$18.95 ($27.95 Canada)

www.humankinetics.com

HUMAN KINETICS
The Premier Publisher for Sports & Fitness
P.O. Box 5076, Champaign, IL 61825-5076